CW01022494

Advanced Introduction to Private International Law and
Procedure

Elgar Advanced Introductions are stimulating and thoughtful introductions to major fields in the social sciences and law, expertly written by the world's leading scholars. Designed to be accessible yet rigorous, they offer concise and lucid surveys of the substantive and policy issues associated with discrete subject areas.

The aims of the series are twofold: to pinpoint essential principles of a particular field, and to offer insights that stimulate critical thinking. By distilling the vast and often technical corpus of information on the subject into a concise and meaningful form, the books serve as accessible introductions for undergraduate and graduate students coming to the subject for the first time. Importantly, they also develop well-informed, nuanced critiques of the field that will challenge and extend the understanding of advanced students, scholars and policy-makers.

For a full list of Edward Elgar published titles, including the titles in this series, visit our website at www.e-elgar.com.

Advanced Introduction to

Private International Law and Procedure

SECOND EDITION

PETER HAY

L.Q.C. Lamar Professor of Law Emeritus, Emory University School of Law, USA

Elgar Advanced Introductions

Cheltenham, UK • Northampton, MA, USA

Published by
Edward Elgar Publishing Limited
The Lypiatts
15 Lansdown Road
Cheltenham
Glos GL50 2JA
UK

Edward Elgar Publishing, Inc.
William Pratt House
9 Dewey Court
Northampton
Massachusetts 01060
USA

A catalogue record for this book
is available from the British Library

Library of Congress Control Number: 2023937062

ISBN 978 1 80392 885 2 (cased)
ISBN 978 1 80392 887 6 (paperback)
ISBN 978 1 80392 886 9 (eBook)

Printed and bound by CPI Group (UK) Ltd, Croydon, CR0 4YY

Contents

Author biography

Peter Hay is L.Q.C. Lamar Professor of Law Emeritus at Emory University in Atlanta and Honorary Professor at the University of Freiberg, Germany. He previously served as Alumni Distinguished Professor of Law at the University of Illinois and as Universitätsprofessor at the University of Dresden (Germany). He has held visiting appointments at Bucerius Law School in Hamburg, the Universities of Bonn and Freiburg, the Central European University in Budapest, and at Stanford Law School. He holds honorary doctorates from Pecs University, Hungary, and Bucerius in Germany. He is a titular member of the International Academy of Comparative Law and a life member of the American Law Institute. He has published widely on Conflict of Laws in American and European journals and is the co-author of the leading American treatise on the subject.

Preface

This book deals with the problems that arise in international litigation in civil and commercial cases. Some are familiar problems (for instance, when does a court have jurisdiction over an out-of-state defendant?), except that the international context adds complexity. Other problems are unique to the settlement of international disputes; for instance, does another country's law apply to the substance of the case, and how does one get a domestic judgment recognized and enforced in a foreign country?

The presentation is problem-oriented and takes a comparative-law approach. The three parts of the book present the principal problems parties face in dealing with cases with an international dimension. The parties who deal with each other may be in different countries, or facts or elements of the case may involve more than the state where suit is brought (the forum state).

There are no international law solutions to these problems, despite the name of the subject of this Advanced Introduction. "Private international law" is the *national law* of each country dealing with *international cases involving private law subject matters.* Answers to the litigation problems identified and discussed in the text may therefore differ somewhat, or even substantially, depending on the national law lens through which these problems are viewed. For this reason, this volume uses a comparative approach.

There are, of course, many nuances in the national laws around the world (see the reference below). But two main "systems" (again with differences within each) stand out, at least in the Western world: the civil law system, derived and developed from Roman law, which is the basis of much of European, South American, and some other legal systems;

and the common law system that spread from England to the United States, Canada, and the British Commonwealth. To narrow things down, this volume compares – in the main, but not exclusively – the law of the European Union as largely representative of civil-law solutions, and the approaches followed in the United States for the common law.

It would be a vast, indeed misleading, overstatement to say that the systems show evidence of converging. Nonetheless, and with problems and the need for solutions being similar, some solutions do resemble each other. As the Conclusions in Chapter 6 suggest, European law has made particular strides in evolving a modern Conflicts law, in some respects adopting some of the flexibility that characterizes American law but doing this in a circumspect and very principled way. Work on the new Restatement (Third) of Conflict of Laws in the United States and the successful elaboration by Hague Conference on Private International Law of a multilateral convention on the recognition and enforcement of judgments may further advance agreement on substantive policies and coordinated or respectful domestic procedures in the not-too-distant future.

Obviously, an Advanced Introduction can only sketch the principal problems and offer a survey of answers and solutions. To keep the text uncluttered, footnotes have been kept to a minimum. References to the important statutory texts of the European Union are given in an Appendix.

Readers who might want to follow up on some topics or study the subject in greater depth may find the following helpful:

- For American law, my co-authored treatise or extensive student study aid:
  - Hay, Borchers, Symeonides, & Whytock, *Conflict of Laws* (6th edition, West Publishing Co. 2018).
  - Hay, *Conflict of Laws – Black Letter Outlines* (9th edition, West Academic Publishing 2023).
- For British law, two classic commentaries:
  - Cheshire, North, & Fawcett, *Private International Law* (15th edition, Oxford University Press 2017).
  - Dicey, Morris, & Collins, *Conflict of Laws* (16th edition, Sweet & Maxwell 2022).
- For an extensive overview:

- Basedow, Rühl, Ferrari, & de Miguel Asension (eds.), *Encyclopedia of Private International Law*, 4 vols. (Vol. 3, with 80 national reports) (Edward Elgar Publishing 2017).

Portions of this text were completed while I was on teaching assignments in Europe, where I also had the benefit of discussions and exchanges with European colleagues, to whom I am grateful. I am also especially grateful to my long-time associate, Daniel J. Levin, J.D., for his helpful review of the final manuscript.

1 Introduction: Basic issues

1.1 "Private International Law"

"Private International Law," as the subject of this book is generally called in civil law countries and often also in the United Kingdom, is really a misnomer. The same is true for "Conflict of Laws," as the subject is called in the United States and many common law countries.

"*Public* International Law" describes the rules – whether by treaty or accepted practice – that apply to how states deal with each other. "*Private* International Law" focusses on the relations of private parties to each other in an international context. But it is not an *international* law that governs these relations: "Private International Law" is the *national* law of each country, applicable to international situations.

"Conflict of Laws" (or "Conflicts" for short, in American usage) suggests competition, a quest for dominance. Yet in many (if not most) cases, the question is rather which of different potentially applicable laws is the most appropriate for the problem at hand. In keeping with modern usage in the English language literature, this book will use "Conflict of Laws" or "conflicts" for want of a more appropriate term.

1.2 The elements of an "international civil case"

This book deals with the main issues involved in litigating a civil case that has international (border-crossing) elements. Consider the following examples. The parties to a contract deal with each other from different countries or, if they are in the same country, their contract calls for performance in another. Or a person from one country injures another in a different country. Or after a divorce, with the ex-spouses now in different countries, issues of child custody, including possible later modification, need to be decided. Or a person dies leaving property in different countries. If he or she left a will, is it valid? If there was none, who inherits?

All of the above examples have in common that an important aspect of the relationship of the parties or of a transaction is in a different country from the one in which suit has been brought or in which the parties acted (for instance, making a contract or a will).

1.2.1   Sources

Conflicts law is basically *national* law. It encompasses both international civil procedure and private international law (choice of law). Unlike public international law (the law applicable to state-to-state relations), it is *not* "international" in its origin or application. Even when a court follows the conflicts rules of another state to determine what substantive law ultimately applies, it does so because its own conflicts law directs it to do so – and not because of some outside mandate. It is even possible that following the conflicts rules of another state could then lead to the application of the substantive law of yet a third state.

Many conflicts rules do derive from international conventions, for instance, those sponsored by the Hague Conference on Private International Law. However, they apply in contracting states only because these states have adopted them as their law, not as a result of any external mandate.

The conflicts rules of the European Union (EU) seem to be an exception: The EU Regulations on jurisdiction and on applicable law do bind the courts of the Member States as directly applicable EU law (except those that exercised their right to opt out in those instances in which such a right was granted), subject to limited recourse to the EU Court of Justice. In this way, EU law resembles federal law, similar to federal law in the United States which overrides the law of the individual states.

Most states of the world have cast their law of international procedure and private international law into national statutory rules, either in individual statutes or in codifications (for the European Union, see above). The states of the United States (as well as many other common law countries, other than Ireland which is subject to EU conflicts rules) follow the case law approach: Applicable decisions rendered by the relevant highest court are precedents and bind lower courts in future cases involving the same issues.

In the United States, the American Law Institute, a private organization of professors, judges, and practitioners, issues "Restatements of the Law" for many areas of the law, including Conflict of Laws. These Restatements summarize and interpret the case law, thereby presenting a national perspective. They are often used, even relied upon, by courts and by the practicing bar. For Conflict of Laws, the current version is the "Restatement (Second)." An American Law Institute working group is currently drafting a "Restatement (Third)," the adoption of which will presumably require at least two more years of additional work. New Restatements do not necessarily replace their predecessors. Rather, they reflect the development of the law, and not all aspects of a given version may need updating or merit further discussion in a subsequent version. Nor do courts necessarily follow the rules of a new Restatement: They may adopt them or prefer other solutions, including those of the older Restatements. The latter thus often remain important resources alongside newer versions.

1.2.2   Issues of an international case: Where to litigate? What law applies?

An international case raises three principal issues that must be considered: (1) where to bring suit (assuming that more than one country could entertain the suit); (2) what law will the court selected by the plaintiff apply (in view of the fact that the case is – by definition – also connected to another country); and finally, (3) if the plaintiff should recover a judgment, where can it be enforced if the defendant has no local assets in the state where the judgment was rendered or if those available are insufficient?

These issues are interrelated so that none can really be addressed in isolation. Selecting the court in which to sue (from among several possible choices) is not just a question of what the plaintiff finds most convenient. Courts in different countries may follow different rules as to what law applies to a particular issue. The *plaintiff* will naturally seek to avoid the possible application of an unfavorable law: the questions to be answered thus concern, first, how a given court will determine what law it will apply and, second, the content of the law that is potentially applicable. Answers to these questions are therefore an important part of the decision where to sue.

In the United States, a *defendant* may also be able to influence what law the court will apply, for instance, by seeking to move the case to another state or country, where a different choice-of-law rule may result in the application of a different substantive law. Cases of dismissal (locally) on the ground of *forum non conveniens* (see 3.7.2) are an example.

Some countries readily recognize and enforce judgments of another country, while other countries impose some preconditions or decline to recognize and enforce particular kinds of judgments. If it is necessary to enforce a judgment against assets in a country other than the one which rendered the judgment, that country's recognition law must also be considered when selecting the court in which to sue in the first place.

This book necessarily treats these three problem areas – where to sue, what law applies, and how to enforce a judgment – in separate sections. But, as the preceding paragraphs point out, their interrelationship should always be kept in mind, inasmuch as an answer to one issue affects the analysis of one or both of the other two.

1.2.3   Scope of coverage

Two of the principal issues – in what court to sue and how to recognize a foreign judgment – deal with procedural questions. With few exceptions, for instance, with respect to some family law matters (see 4.6.1), courts apply the law of their own country to these procedural questions. Although such questions may be treated differently in different legal systems, the approach of a given system generally applies regardless of the subject matter of the dispute.

This is not so when it comes to the question of what law applies, as the question is not purely procedural. Here, the question requires nuanced analysis to determine whether the law of the court's own country (the "*lex fori*") or that of another legal system should be applied.

This book addresses questions of the applicable law with regard to the main areas of private law: contract, tort, property, family law, and succession. It does not deal with areas for which there is uniform substantive law, in particular international sales, to which the Vienna (UN) Convention on the International Sale of Goods (CISG)[1] applies. This book also does not address insolvency. On the procedural side, non-judicial remedies (arbitration and methods of alternative dispute resolution) are also excluded.

As the discussion has already shown, conflicts law – like the national law of each state – is not uniform. Even when the problems presented by international cases are the same or alike, different national laws sometimes deal with them differently. This book attempts to give the reader a comparative overview. Of course, there are limits to what may be addressed comprehensively, so this book therefore focusses on American law (as representing the common law) and on the law of the EU (as representing perhaps the most modern solutions that have evolved in civil law systems). For American law, the book also considers the current work on the Restatement (Third), mentioned earlier. For the source of EU law, see 4.1.2. An appendix provides citations to some of the principal EU statutory materials ("Regulations").

1.2.4   A note on terminology: the different meanings of "jurisdiction"

"Jurisdiction" appears throughout any discussion of conflicts law. But the term carries different meanings, depending on the context. One general meaning of "jurisdiction" – also used in non-conflicts law settings – is simply as a synonym for "courts," "states," or "legal systems" other than one's own, as in a statement such as "In some jurisdictions, the rule is ..."

More important for present purposes is the use of "jurisdiction" as defining the power of a legislative or judicial body. "Legislative jurisdiction," as the term itself indicates, concerns the existence and extent of power of a body (legislature, administrative agency with rule-making authority) to make laws or other binding rules. In contrast, "jurisdiction to adjudicate"

---

[1]   United Nations Convention on contracts for the international sale of goods, April 11, 1980, 1489 U.N.T.S. 3.

refers to the power of courts or, again, of administrative units to render binding decisions in specific cases.

As we consider a court's "power to adjudicate," we distinguish further between its "subject matter jurisdiction" and the concept of "personal jurisdiction." The former concerns the authority of a court to adjudicate substantive matters of a certain type. For example, a family court does not generally deal with matters of insolvency. The latter describes the power of a court to affect the rights and duties of the parties before it. For example, under what circumstances does a court have the power to impose an obligation on a non-resident party? Section 3.3 deals extensively with this latter aspect: a court's power to reach and bind the parties.

1.3   Applicable law and the goals of conflicts law

1.3.1   In general

The goal of all law and its application (judging) is to achieve "justice," perhaps best defined as results that reflect the values and norms of the particular civilization and its era. These norms may be religious or secular in origin. For the decision of a legal dispute, it is necessary to determine where to find the relevant norms and whether they apply to the case at hand. In international cases, more than one value system and set of norms may be relevant. This presents the difficult task of how to choose – between or among them, or even to accommodate more than one, all in order to achieve "justice." A brief look at the history of conflicts law recalls how this question has been answered over time. This look will help in understanding and dealing with today's answers, in particular the difference in approach between European-oriented conflicts law and that of the United States.

1.3.2   Historical notes

Today's conflicts law still contains some elements dating back to Roman law, for instance, that a person's domicile, defined as the person's relation to a territory, supplied the "personal law." That law applied to such questions as capacity and citizenship. The law of the *situs* (the location of a thing), in contrast, determined the rights in the thing, whether movable or immovable. The vast expanse of the Roman Empire at that time and the bestowal of citizenship on inhabitants of newly acquired territories did not make for any real conflicts cases. Such cases arose with the later emergence of the city states: they had rules of law of their own and needed to decide which law applied. In the Classical period, it was only to non-Romans that different law applied. It was administered by a special official, the *praetor peregrinus*, who fashioned it from universal, natural law principles and traditions, the *ius gentium* (the "law of peoples," later "law of nations") – origin of today's public international law.

In the city states, emerging conflicts problems were addressed by classifying legal rules (*statuta*) as "personal," following and applying to the citizen wherever he was, and as "real," applicable only in the territory of the enacting state. Some of the resulting classifications strike us as mechanical and arbitrary today. The great modern conflicts methodologies all rejected the *statuta* approach, but in many cases arrived at similar results in their own fashion.

We find notions of *territoriality* in some form in virtually all approaches to choice of law – since the days of *Ulrich Huber*, the seventeenth-century Dutch jurist, considered by many to be the "father" of modern conflicts law, to *Carl Georg von Wächter* and *Friedrich Carl von Savigny* in Germany and *Joseph Story* in America in the nineteenth century, to *Brainerd Currie* and to the first (and to some extent the second) American Restatement in the twentieth century. *Huber* taught that laws apply to all persons within the territory where established, but also limited to it. However, "comity," the respect nations should have for each other, should lead to application of a foreign law to protect rights acquired under it. Both *Savigny* and *Story*, the founders of conflicts in their respective countries, forcefully embraced the idea of comity as a guiding principle. On the other hand, *Wächter* rejected the idea and advocated the application of forum law in most cases. In this approach, often overlooked, he was really a forerunner of *Brainerd Currie* in the 1950s in the United States (see 4.3.3.1). *Huber's* concern with rights acquired in a place other than the forum became the "vested rights" school of thought, enshrined in the first American Restatement.

Territoriality was the focus of all of the foregoing: to refer to a specific place (state, country) for choosing the law to apply to the case at hand. It was like sticking a pin in a map. Other aspects of the case, such as the relation of the parties to each other, or the fact that the actual home of the parties was in yet another state (where the effects of the decision would be felt), were not considered. How the relevant "place" of the applicable law was to be determined was refined over time. *Savigny* was the first to seek to identify the (territorial) "seat of the legal relationship" that was in issue in a case. This approach was further refined by the American Second Restatement over a century later: It now seeks to determine (in contract and tort) the place to which an issue has "the most significant relationship," in light of some guiding principles that it suggests. Many recent conflicts codifications, among them the Choice of Law Regulations of the EU, seek to provide predictability – by establishing specific choice-of-law rules for particular case categories – and at the same time allow for some flexibility when another law is "manifestly more closely connected" to the case at hand. The latter reference thus seeks a territorial solution to a relationship in the *Savigny* and Second Restatement sense.

Only some scholars advocated practically abandoning, or at least very much limiting, all territorial orientation. The "better law" approach, adopted by five states in the United States for torts conflicts cases (two of them also for contracts cases), clearly does that. Similarly, the idea that the determination of the applicable law must be the result of a "consequences-based" approach, advocated by *Russell J. Weintraub* in the United States, would of course lead to a (territorial) law, but not assign importance to the element of territoriality. With the limited exception just noted in connection with the "better law" approach, these suggestions have not taken hold, in the sense of freeing courts from rules to let them be guided by their own value judgments.

To some extent, "governmental interest analysis" (see 4.3.3.1) seeks to address, perhaps to weigh, factors and elements other than the territorial connection of the case. However, as will be seen later, this approach as well as the "better law" approach (as applied in practice), often lead homeward – that is, they direct application of the *lex fori* – and thereby substitute one territorial law for another.

All modern codifications of conflicts law, such as in the EU (and as distinguished from the American case law approach), start with a rule orientation. Against that backdrop, they provide for exceptions and, with them, the flexibility needed to prevent unjust consequences. The exceptions are necessarily formulated before any individual case or dispute; they reflect the legislator's value judgments. There is no built-in homeward trend, and *ad hoc* decisions are minimized.

The approaches to choice of law briefly reviewed above are reflected in various and different ways and to different degrees in all modern legal systems. (See also 4.1 and following. Should the treatment in that section seem confusing, it may prove helpful to review this overview.)

The territorial orientation for dealing with international cases is, of course, understandable when the issue is whether local courts have juris- diction to entertain such cases. The reach of the jurisdiction of a local court is defined by and parallels the reach of its own law – originally, the whole Roman Empire; later, only the particular city state; today, the nation state or regional state-like arrangement, such as the EU. Major changes have occurred over time regarding the *extraterritorial* reach of a forum court – both to apply local law to citizens now living abroad (for instance, universal taxation), as well as to draw in foreign defendants in cases where their acts or conduct have produced local effects (for instance, violation of the forum's antitrust laws). Such an extended reach of judicial jurisdiction does not occur by itself; it accompanies the forum state's asserted extraterritorial reach of its law. That is, it applies in tandem with the forum state's claim to assert regulatory power beyond its borders. Part I of this book deals with the exercise of adjudicatory jurisdiction.

1.3.3   The older European model – rule orientation to achieve "conflicts justice"

Roman law influenced much of Continental European (and even some English) law through the nineteenth century and into the early twentieth century. It was supplemented or adapted to a greater or lesser extent, depending on the country, by local statutes, ordinances, custom, or usage. The nineteenth century brought the beginning of the great codifications of private law. The first was Napoleon's Civil Code in France 1806, fol- lowed by the Austrian Civil Code of 1811, and the German Civil Code in 1900.

Conflicts law also became codified, for instance, as the Introductory Statute of the German Civil Code. These statutes provided concrete rules for such questions as the law applicable to tort, the validity of a contract, the capacity to contract, or the capacity to marry, among many others.

These rules represented value judgments by the law-maker as to what law should be most appropriately applied to achieve a (perceived) just (right) result. These rules were thus based on abstract value judgments – judgments made in advance, without regard to any particular concrete case. As a result, rigid application of a rule could result in hardship in a particular case.

Take the case of parties from State A, whose cars collide in State B. The conflicts rule in State A, where one of the parties sues the other, refers to the law of the place of injury (State B) for the calculation of damages. B law provides for much less than A law, yet it is in State A that the plaintiff suffers the effects of the accident, and possibly incurs medical expenses that B law does not compensate. Should such a circumstance permit an exception? Should a court be allowed to make adjustments?

To allow this would enable the court to reach a *substantively* just result, as the court sees it, even if this means unequal application of conflicts rules from case to case. The opposing view, favored by the German conflicts scholar *Gerhard Kegel*, regards conflicts law like any other body of law, with justice demanding equal application. Such "conflicts justice" requires an internally coherent system, not allowing for *ad hoc* administration in the interest of "substantive justice."[2] To this school, "substantive justice" would require reform of substantive law by the legislator, but not judicial adjustments of conflicts law.

Concern with "substantive justice" could nonetheless be addressed at times, even within the traditional system. For instance, if it were possible to consider a claim as arising from a contract issue rather than from a tort issue (or some other such switch in labels), a different conflicts norm would apply, and might lead to a different law. Similarly, if something could be regarded as a procedural issue (to which forum law applies), application of a conflicts norm leading to an undesirable substantive law could be avoided.[3] These, then, were "escapes" from the strict system without, however, making basic changes or adjustments in it.

---

[2]   Gerhard Kegel & Klaus Schurig, *Internationales Privatrecht* § 2 (Munich: CH Beck Verlag, 9th ed., 2004).

[3]   This labeling of subject matter and issues is called "characterization" or "qualification." For further discussion, see 4.3.4.1.

1.3.4   The American conflicts "revolution"

American private law is the law of the individual states, and so are the approaches to choice of the applicable law. Each interstate (across-state lines) case is therefore a conflicts case, the same as a case involving a foreign country. Choice-of-law considerations appropriate for an American interstate case do not necessarily satisfy the needs of international situations, yet existing law draws few distinctions – and revisions may not either.

American conflicts law – with the exception of two states, one territory, and a few statutory rules in others – is not codified. It is case law, the same as most substantive areas of private law. Judicial precedents govern, and, because of the state-law nature of conflicts law, these may well differ from state to state. In the past, there was a high degree of uniformity, as older judicial precedents established definite rules. Examples include applying the law of the place of commission of a tort for redress, or that the validity of a contract was determined according to the law of the place of contracting. The underlying theory was that rights and obligations "vested" at a certain time and place. Identifying the place geographically for the relevant time automatically provided the applicable law. These rules differed little from state to state.

Achieving just results within the rigid structure of the traditional rule-based system, essentially through the use of "escape" devices, still proved difficult, and produced too many artificial, unsatisfactory results. Many voices called for reforms, especially in the United States. In contrast to the *First Restatement of Conflict of Laws* (1932), which embodied the rules of the traditional approach, a number of important contributions presented models for change. These ranged from establishing "principles of preference" (*David F. Cavers*) or "choice-influencing considerations" (*Robert A. Leflar*) for choice of law, to the very influential emphasis on "governmental interests" (*Brainerd Currie*), an often inward-looking approach that will be considered in greater detail later (see 4.3.3.1). In 1971, the *Restatement (Second) of Conflict of Laws* attempted to do more than restate; it also sought to provide an accommodation of the several divergent views. At the same time, it retained traditional rules for some subject areas, in which certainty and predictability were particularly important factors (for instance, in the law of property and of decedents' estates). Its success in achieving a workable accommodation (for instance, with the adoption of a vaguely defined "most significant relationship" test for choice of law in tort and contract) was limited, as discussed below in further detail (see 4.3.3.3). Currently, work is under way in the American Law Institute – the influential private organization with judges, academics and practitioners as members – which promulgates Restatements for many areas of law, to draft a *Restatement (Third) of Conflict of Laws*. It may be finished and released in another two or three years' time.[4]

1.3.4.1   *Excursus: the American parallel court system*

In the context of the above, it should be recalled that there is a parallel system of state and federal courts in every state of the United States. The courts of both systems have subject-matter jurisdiction in most civil and commercial matters. Exceptions are, for instance, bankruptcy (only federal courts) and family law (state courts). Despite their concurrent subject-matter jurisdiction, access to a federal court requires either that (1) the plaintiff has alleged a violation of federal law (a "federal question"); or that (2) the parties have different state or national citizenship ("diversity of citizenship") and the amount in controversy exceeds $75,000.

Private law, including conflicts law, is mostly state law, as mentioned earlier. The highest authority for state private law is a state's highest court (except when state law conflicts with federal law, which takes precedence). When a federal court exercises its diversity of citizenship jurisdiction in a matter of private law, it applies the choice-of-law doctrine of the state in which it sits. Such doctrine guides the court's determination of the law applicable to the subject matter of the dispute. Thus, federal courts are bound by the choice-of-law precedents of their local state's highest court, as well as the precedents of the highest court of the state that provides the law applicable to the subject matter of the dispute. Changes in conflicts law and methodology therefore come from the state court system.

1.3.5   Modern approaches and trends

1.3.5.1   *United States*

In the United States, work has begun on a *Restatement (Third) of Conflict of Laws*, as mentioned above. It will bring more certainty by providing

---

[4]   See 4.3.3.5. For extensive discussion, see Peter Hay, "On the Road to a Third American Restatement of Conflicts Law," 42 *Praxis des Internationalen Privat- und Verfahrensrechts* [IPRax] 205 (2022).

(i.e., proposing for adoption by the courts) some more definite "rules," while guiding courts with detailed lists of contacts and policy considerations in their decision to select the applicable law in cases for which no rules have been suggested. However, not evident so far is whether sufficient attention is being paid to the needs of international (foreign country) conflicts cases, as distinguished from interstate cases.

Civil procedure is also state law, but subject to federal constitutional limitations, in particular, the Due Process Clause of the Federal Constitution's Fourteenth Amendment. As interpreted by the United States Supreme Court, interstate and international cases are largely treated alike, leading to some perplexing results. A striking example was a ruling that an English manufacturer of a product, which it marketed in the United States generally, was not subject to personal jurisdiction in the state in which its product injured the plaintiff because it had not itself introduced the product directly into that particular state (see further 3.3.2).

1.3.5.2   Europe

EU legislation has been remarkably successful in providing certainty through definite rules. This is so with regard to both rules of procedure and choice-of-law rules. These rules also establish policy-guided, defined exceptions: the latter as part of the rule rather than by judicial decision in the individual case as in the United States. The exceptions acknowledge that courts must be permitted to depart from strictly defined rules in the individual exceptional case (escape clauses). The fact that the rule itself establishes the circumstances under which a departure from it is appropriate also means that courts are not to render individualized, *ad hoc* decisions. This methodology of EU conflicts law is now reflected in the codifications or revisions of older conflicts law in other countries as well (see 6.3).

1.3.5.3   Elsewhere

New codifications of private international law abound (see 6.3). Especially, Eastern European countries have adopted new or revised older private international law codifications. Major work has been undertaken in the People's Republic of China.[5] All have adopted rules (in the civil law tradition), but have introduced flexibility through pre-formulated, policy-based exceptions, in the manner demonstrated by EU legislation. All of them address the extent to which the parties may choose the applicable law (party autonomy). The rules may be broad and general, limited by exceptions, or they may be narrow from the beginning. Rules and their exceptions of course reflect the political and social values of the enacting country: They cannot be generalized. At best, there are trends that can be noted, as subsequent discussion will show.

1.4   Connecting factors

When does a state assert jurisdiction to adjudicate a claim? When does a court apply another state's law or prefer its own? The answers depend on how the particular international case is related to the court's own or to another state: What connects the case to this or another state? All legal systems resort to the same "connecting factors" to answer these questions, but the relevance or appropriateness of these factors differs and depends on the context in which they are used. A person's home (his or her *domicile*, in the Anglo-American sense, or *habitual residence*, now the more usual civil law reference) may be the proper connecting factor for all suits against him or her. They may also be appropriate for the choice of the applicable law in family law and inheritance contexts, while the place of the commission of a delict (tort), elsewhere than at the defendant's home, may be appropriate both for jurisdiction over the claim and for the law to be applied to it. On the other hand, domicile may be inappropriate as a connecting factor for other matters, such as a claim for the breach of a contract concluded elsewhere. What connecting factors legal systems use and how broadly or narrowly they define them will be explored in the substantive contexts below.

---

[5]   The Choice of Law Act of 2010 provides a more-or-less general framework for Chinese conflicts law. The several Interpretations of the Supreme People's Court, beginning with the first in 2012, provide the operative rules in practice. See Qingkun Xu, "The Codification of Conflicts Law in China: A Long Way to Go," 65 Am. J. Comp. L. 919 (2017).

Connecting factors are not interrelated; in other words, satisfaction for one purpose, say for the question of jurisdiction, does not automatically mean satisfaction for another purpose, such as the question of what law applies. Example: a court may well have jurisdiction over the defendant, for instance, because the defendant is domiciled in the state, but application of local law (the *lex fori*) may be inappropriate because all aspects of the claim involved in the case are connected to another state or country. That is why the American Restatement (Second) refers to the law of the state that has the "most significant relationship" to an issue (see 4.3.3.3), or the proposed Restatement (Third) to "the most appropriate law" or the law of the state with the "dominant interest." Similarly, Article 2 of the Chinese Choice of Law Act 2010 refers to the "closest connection," a reference first used in contract cases.

PART I

Jurisdiction to adjudicate

2   Forum-selection clauses

2.1   Prorogation and derogation

As mentioned in Chapter 1 (and described further below), plaintiffs can often choose among several places where they might bring suit. Of course, the same also holds true the other way around: a party might be sued in one of several places. Parties will often seek certainty, especially to have all suits against them by all potential plaintiffs be brought in the same forum: they seek to avoid being sued in multiple possible places with respect to essentially similar claims. They may therefore seek inclusion of a forum-selection clause in their agreements, designating a single court or two alternative courts as the one(s) to hear disputes that may arise between them and their contracting party.

A forum-selection clause has two effects. First, it gives jurisdiction to the designated court, which it otherwise might not have under its law: The parties voluntarily submit to it in advance (prorogation). Second, at the same time, the parties mean to take jurisdiction away (derogation) from all courts that might otherwise have been able to assert jurisdiction. As a result, the selected court usually is intended to have exclusive jurisdiction. Whether the derogated court will honor the derogation, though so intended by the parties, is for that court to decide if a party sues there in violation of the agreement (see also Section 2.2.5). Of course, the parties cannot give a court jurisdiction over a subject within the exclusive jurisdiction of another court. For instance, the parties cannot give jurisdiction to a court in State A over real property located in State B, as the court of the location (situs) has exclusive jurisdiction.

2.2   Some limits

The parties' freedom is not unfettered. For instance, does it matter whether the transaction involves a "weaker" party, such as a consumer, an employee, or an insured? May the parties select a court that has no relation to the parties or the transaction? Would it matter that the chosen court would not apply a regulatory law of the derogated state that the latter feels strongly about (for instance, rules of antitrust law)? Are there requirements of form (for instance, a writing, an electronic communication)? There are considerable differences among legal systems regarding possible limitations. In the present context, who decides on the validity of a forum-selection clause?

2.2.1   EU law

At first blush, the general provision of EU law applicable to forum-selection clauses (the "Brussels Ia" Regulation) appears to be one of the most liberal: Parties from within or without the EU may designate a Member State court to have exclusive jurisdiction. Note, however, that the provision is limited to the choice of a Member State court. The choice of a non-EU court remains a matter of the national law of each of the Member States, and their laws do differ. Furthermore, other provisions of EU law protect "weaker" parties: Consumers, insureds, and employees may be sued only in the states of their domicile. A different forum selection is valid only if concluded *after* a concrete dispute has arisen. A forum selection needs to be in writing, in an electronic form that can be preserved, or in a "form which accords with usage [in international trade or commerce]" of which the parties were or should have been aware. The last of these, while commercially highly desirable, may of course also be the source of controversy.

The national laws of EU Member States differ. One example is the way that they protect weaker parties to a contract. Another is the way that they guard against misuse, such as when a forum-selection clause becomes part of a contract as part of a party's "General Conditions." Illustratively, German law imposes no restrictions on forum-selection agreements concluded by "merchants" (as defined by German commercial law). However, it achieves the EU law's weaker party protection in agreements with a non-merchant by not permitting a pre-dispute forum selection unless one of the parties is not subject to general jurisdiction domestically. In addition, the general validity of standardized "General Conditions" with consumers (non-merchants) is subject to statutory limits established by §§ 307 and 310 of the German Civil Code (for instance, no unliquidated damage or penalty clauses are allowed).

2.2.2   The Hague Convention

The Choice of Court Convention of the Hague Conference of International Law,[1] in force in the EU but only in a few other countries, imposes broader restrictions. Greater limits result from the fact that the Convention may potentially have worldwide effect, compared with EU law that is applicable in and to a more cohesive group of states. Thus, the Convention's provisions are mainly concerned with effective judicial relief in the chosen forum and with the question whether suit in a non-chosen (derogated) forum, which is opposed to the clause on public policy grounds, is an appropriate reason for not honoring the choice (see 2.2.4).

2.2.3   United States

In the United States, initial hostility to the derogation effect of forum-selection clauses has given way to their widespread acceptance. All except about three states have followed the United States Supreme Court's lead (in a federal decision that does not control state law cases[2]) and honor such clauses, in particular when the chosen forum is in some way related to the transaction or there appears some good reason for its choice (for instance, its expertise with respect to particular cases, such as England in maritime matters). Weaker party protection may be achieved by rejecting a forum selection as "unreasonable," for instance, when a consumer contract between Louisiana parties stipulated for jurisdiction of Italian courts.[3]

2.2.4   Rejecting a choice

Despite a general acceptance of forum-selection clauses, a court may still refuse to honor such a clause in a particular case when implementing it would violate the public policy of the forum (possibly even that of another

---

[1]   Convention on Choice of Court Agreements, June 30, 2005, 44 I.L.M. 1294.
[2]   *M/S Bremen v. Zapata Off-Shore Co.*, 407 U.S. 1 (1972).
[3]   Ibid.

state). Public policy is a rather generic concept (also discussed further below, in connection with choice of the applicable law). In the present context, the forum court may fear that the chosen court, to which it is asked to defer, may not apply the same law that it would apply, which it is persuaded *must* be applied. Such application would therefore be evaded if the case were dismissed in favor of another forum. What is at issue are what European law calls "overriding mandatory norms." Every state has such norms, the most obvious example being norms of antitrust law that the forum would apply to foreigners, acting abroad, whose conduct restrains trade or has other anticompetitive effects in the forum. A foreign court might well not apply the present forum's norms, but the present forum feels compelled, as a matter of local public policy, to ensure the enforcement of forum mandatory norms, if need be, by keeping the case and not honoring the selection of another forum. A number of American decisions (involving arbitration) have enforced arbitration clauses even when it was unclear what law would be applied. However, they did voice concern, in some cases, that mandatory norms of forum law might not be honored by the foreign forum, and therefore signaled the possibility of review of the foreign court's action in the future, for instance, at the time when an award is brought back for enforcement. Other jurisdictions may reject forum selection clauses on grounds of local public policy more readily; there are, after all, no truly objective standards as to when something rises to the level of an "overriding" (local) mandatory norm.

2.2.5   Breach of a forum-selection clause

When a dispute arises, one of the parties may decide to ignore the forum-selection clause and initiate suit in another forum (for reasons of convenience, more favorable procedural law, or whatever). The party thereby breaches its contractual obligation. As discussed earlier (2.1), the court in which suit is brought (the derogated court) should enforce the clause and dismiss the suit, unless the clause itself must be disregarded on the basis of one of the limits discussed above. Assuming that the clause was valid and the suit is to be dismissed, its disregard also constituted a breach of contract which might have caused the injured party losses and costs (for instance, litigation expenses in the derogated court). Does the injured party have a cause of action for contract damages? The German Supreme Court so held in 2019: the "dual nature" of a forum-selection clause (procedural and contractual) supported a contract remedy. This result should discourage circumventing otherwise valid forum-selection clauses. The United States has not yet expressly embraced it, although the Supreme Court has directed lower courts to give the greatest possible weight to the parties' contractual agreement. It stopped short of giving it the same overriding effect as it does to party agreement to arbitrate.[4]

2.2.6   The law applicable to a forum-selection clause

What law applies to the validity and interpretation of a forum-selection clause? A number of American decisions hold expressly that it is the law that governs the substance of the dispute, whether determined by a choice-of-law clause, or absent such a clause, by the forum's choice-of-law rules. This means that the forum selection may well be governed by a law other than that of the forum where the case was brought.

Civil law jurisdictions, and particularly EU law, are more express. They regard the stipulation selecting the forum to be *separate* from the substantive parts of the agreement. The former is governed by the law of the chosen forum, and the latter by whatever law applies as a matter of conflicts law. If the agreement also contains a choice-of-law clause, its validity would need to be determined first (for which, see 4.2.1). If valid, then the chosen law supplies the law by which to judge the forum-selection clause; if not, then the forum's conflicts law will determine which law applies.

The inquiries into the validity of the choice-of-forum clause and the substantive contract itself may therefore be different: A forum selection may turn out to be valid, while the main contract may turn out not to be valid under the substantive law applicable to it. In the reverse case, that is, if the chosen court holds the forum-selection clause to be invalid, that court thereby declares that it lacks jurisdiction to rule on the substance. The plaintiff must then seek redress in a court that has jurisdiction in the absence of a forum-selection clause.

With regard to civil law jurisdictions in particular, the above must be qualified in light of the discussion in 2.2.4: Possibly negative mandatory rules of forum law will apply, and potentially overcome contrary rules of the chosen forum. The same is true in the United States when the forum's

---

[4]   For full discussion, see Peter Hay, "Forum Selection Clauses – Procedural Tools or Contractual Obligations?", 40 *Praxis des Internationalen Privat- und Verfahrensrechts* [IPRax] 505 (2020).

mandatory rule overcomes the law of another jurisdiction that would otherwise apply.

2.3   One-sided clauses

2.3.1   Adhesion provisions

A forum-selection clause may be one-sided and burdensome for the party obligated by it. General limitations on the freedom to negotiate such clauses, designed to protect consumers, should ordinarily take care of this problem, as discussed earlier. However, in at least one case,[5] the United States Supreme Court was not concerned that an adhesion contract contained a forum-selection clause: The weaker party had notice (or the opportunity to inform him or herself), and the clause was standard practice in the particular industry.

2.3.2   Clauses excluding recourse to court

A particular practice of resorting to one-sided clauses, currently very much in vogue in the United States, deserves additional brief mention: Stipulations often require one party (the consumer) to submit any future dispute to individual arbitration (excluding recourse to courts), while the other party may remain free either to resort to arbitration or to sue. Such a stipulation bars recourse to the courts, including by class action (which is often the only financially possible way for weaker parties to pursue claims), and also prohibits class arbitration. Some civil law legal systems (for instance, the German) explicitly preclude parties from excluding judicial recourse in advance of an actual dispute. By necessary implication (see 2.2.1), so does EU law. In the United States, the Federal Supreme Court has upheld such stipulations as consistent with the federal policy favoring arbitration.[6] That policy of course supports the enforceability of an agreement to arbitrate an existing dispute. Due process concerns, however, may speak against surrendering judicial relief for any and all future disputes, especially in an adhesion contract setting. Even apart

---

5   *Carnival Cruise Lines, Inc. v. Shute*, 499 U.S. 585 (1991).
6   For full discussion, see Peter Hay, "Forum Selection Clauses – Procedural Tools or Contractual Obligations?", 40 *Praxis des Internationalen Privat- und Verfahrensrechts* [IPRax] 505 (2020).

from this, compulsory arbitration disadvantages weaker parties who face high costs but cannot combine with like claimants. Several law firms, through use of social media, combined and encouraged claimants to contact them and then filed individual arbitration notices for all who responded. One major American company, thus faced with thousands of arbitration requests, according to newspaper reports, thereupon dropped its mandatory arbitration clauses in contracts with its customers in 2021.[7]

---

[7]   The company involved was Amazon. See *New York Times*, July 22, 2021, updated September 28, 2021.

3 Jurisdiction over persons and things

3.1 *In rem* jurisdiction

It makes a difference whether a plaintiff seeks a determination that he or she has a right *in* a thing (i.e., a right *in rem*: for instance, that he or she is the *owner* of a particular object, such as a painting or a piece of real property) or whether he or she seeks a decision establishing his or her right *to* a thing. An example of the latter is the claim that he or she, and not the defendant, is entitled to have the thing, and that the defendant, who now owns it, should hand it over. In the first case, *the thing* is the object of the litigation; in the second, the litigation is about *the obligation* (or lack of it) that the litigants owe to each other. For the first case, the court needs to have jurisdiction *over the thing* (the thing must be physically subject to its power): The court at the situs (location of the thing) has *in rem* jurisdiction ("over the thing"). In the second type of case – when the issue is the relationship of the parties to each other (for instance, an obligation to deliver a particular thing or to convey land), the court lacks jurisdiction over the absent object of the claim but could issue a binding order (to be given effect by a court where the object, the thing, is located). For that, the court needs jurisdiction over *the person of the defendant* (*in personam* jurisdiction). Sections 3.2 to 3.7 deal with the prerequisites and other issues relating to a court's assertion of *personal* (*in personam*) jurisdiction. For further, more detailed, discussion of *in rem* jurisdiction, see 3.8.

3.2   General personal jurisdiction

When a person may be sued on any claim – without regard to whether the claim is related to the forum state – the court is said to exercise *general jurisdiction*. It is not the connection of the claim, but the close connection of the defendant to the forum state that gives the court such broad personal jurisdiction. In earlier times, forum state nationality of the defendant would permit the forum state to proceed against him or her on claims not related to the forum, even if the defendant was presently absent from the forum. Nationality continues to be a basis for general jurisdiction in many countries; however, in an increasing number of other states, it has been replaced by a person's domicile or habitual residence. This is true both in the EU and in the United States, although there are differences between the Anglo-American definition of domicile and the more objective reference of the civil law (see 4.3.5.1).

3.2.1   Exorbitant rules

In common law jurisdictions like the United States, general jurisdiction may also be based on the mere fact that the papers instituting suit were served on the defendant while he or she was only casually present, perhaps only passing through the forum state ("transient jurisdiction").

"Transient jurisdiction" favors the local plaintiff; he or she can draw in the defendant (sue at home) rather than sue at the latter's domicile. Probably all legal systems have some plaintiff-favoring rule. German law used to permit the exercise of general jurisdiction (now narrowed by judicial construction) when the defendant had some/any property in Germany; a relation of the property to the claim was not then required. French law permits a plaintiff to sue a foreigner on the basis of the plaintiff's French citizenship. These claim-unrelated assertions of jurisdiction have also been termed "exorbitant" because they seem to overreach when neither the defendant nor the claim has a forum state connection.

No exorbitant bases may be invoked in an EU national court against a defendant domiciled in a Member State (Brussels Ia Regulation, Art. 5(2)). The present common law member of the EU – Ireland – therefore may not invoke general jurisdiction against an EU defendant on the basis of transient jurisdiction. However, it may retain the concept as against third-country defendants. The 2019 Hague Convention on the Recognition and Enforcement of Foreign Judgments in Civil and Commercial Matters, to which the EU has acceded for all of its Member States and which enters into force on September 1, 2023, excludes recognition of another member country's decision if the service of the documents instituting the suit violates the public policy of the recognizing country. "Transient service" and jurisdiction based on the plaintiff's citizenship violate the public policy of most countries.

A final exorbitant basis of jurisdiction is "jurisdiction by necessity." On this basis, a country's law may permit a court to exercise jurisdiction when the plaintiff cannot find another court with jurisdiction, or when conditions in the other state (e.g., civil unrest, corrupt courts) really do not provide adequate access to justice. An example of this is Article 7 of the EU's Maintenance Regulation, providing for jurisdiction of a Member State court with "sufficient connection to the dispute" when no other Member State court has jurisdiction under the Regulation and it would be "impossible" for the creditor to sue in a third state. Apart from the obvious interest of the forum in providing its plaintiff with legal recourse, it might still be debatable why the defendant should bear the burden, contrary to the usual concern for balance and fairness.

3.2.2   Jurisdiction over companies

What is an appropriate analogy to a natural person's domicile for the determination of when there is a basis for general jurisdiction over a business entity? EU law offers three options: the place of a company's "statutory seat;" the place of its central administration; or its principal place of business. "Statutory seat" is a civil law concept (*siège réel*) and refers to the company's (main) registered office as named in its founding instrument (the *statut*). The 2019 Hague Convention on Judgment Recognition adds the state of the company's central management. These overlap with the usual references used in common law countries (for instance, place of incorporation in the United States and the United Kingdom; principal place of business in the United States) and such civil law concepts as a company's seat (which may or may not coincide with one of the foregoing).

American law used to have an additional, very broad, basis (as it does for natural persons with the "transient jurisdiction" concept): It permitted the exercise of general jurisdiction wherever the company did "continuous and systematic business." In the case of large national companies, this could literally be everywhere in the United States. In 2011, the United States Supreme Court struck down such an extensive interpretation and application.[1] Now, a company needs to have a qualitatively closer connection to the state (it must be "at home" there) before that state may exercise general jurisdiction. It remains unclear how close the connection needs to be to satisfy the "at home" test, except that the author of the opinion in a subsequent case[2] stated that the "at home" test did not necessarily limit the exercise of general jurisdiction to the state of incorporation or of the corporation's principal place of business.

3.3   Specific (or special) jurisdiction

As was seen, there are relatively limited circumstances when a court can exercise general jurisdiction over a defendant when the plaintiff's claim has no relation to the forum state. This is to protect the defendant against harassment, i.e., being hauled into court where he or she could not expect it. At the same time, it is not always fair to restrict the plaintiff to having to sue at the defendant's domicile or principal place of business. The concept of "specific jurisdiction" accommodates the interests of both plaintiff and defendant: When the plaintiff's claim arises from a contact that the defendant established or otherwise had with a state, it is fair to let the plaintiff bring suit in that state and to require the defendant to answer there. The simplest example is a car accident that a non-resident defendant causes in the plaintiff's state. The plaintiff may of course always sue the defendant in the latter's home state. But for claims arising out of the accident, he or she may sue in the state of the accident; the court there exercises jurisdiction specific (and limited) to claims arising from the accident. Specific jurisdiction thus is *claim-related jurisdiction*, while general jurisdiction focusses only upon the relationship of the defendant to the forum state, no matter what the claim is.

---

[1]   *Goodyear Dunlop Tires Operations, S.A. v. Brown*, 564 U.S. 915 (2011).
[2]   *Daimler AG v. Bauman*, 571 U.S. 117 (2014).

3.3.1   What contacts confer specific jurisdiction?

What does it mean that the claim must "arise from or be related to" the defendant's contact with the forum state? The answer is easy when it is a claim directly connected with an act of the defendant; the damage action for the car accident in the previous paragraph is such a case. So is a contract claim when the contract was to be performed (EU law) or perhaps also made (United States law) in the forum. The matter becomes more difficult when the claim *relates* to the defendant's contact but does not directly arise from it. What if a party wishes to sue another for unfair competition (a tort claim) on the basis of a breach of a distributorship contract made and to be performed within the forum state? In this example, claims are intertwined: The tort claim relates to the contractual relation (indeed, it would not exist without it), but it does not seek damages for breach of contract but for some injury arising from the tort.

In the United States, many individual states in the past had so-called "long-arm statutes" that specified those forum-contacts that justified the state's "reaching out," as it were, and requiring the defendant to answer in the forum state. The EU follows this model in its jurisdiction law and specifies for what claims and under what circumstances a non-resident EU defendant may be sued in the local forum. These cases of specific jurisdiction are regarded as special and as exceptions to the rules on general jurisdiction. In the view of the EU Court of Justice, they are therefore to be construed narrowly; the specific jurisdiction for contract would not support jurisdiction for the tort claim in the example in the preceding paragraph.

In the United States, long-arm statutes have given way to non-specific formulations, such as statutory provisions permitting the exercise of jurisdiction "to the limits of due process" (the federal constitutional limitation on courts acting extraterritorially). These "limits" are exceeded, in the language of an old leading United States Supreme Court decision, when the defendant and the claim did not have "minimum contacts" with the forum or, in another formulation, when the defendant (in connection with the claim) did not "avail himself" of forum benefits. What constitutes "minimum contacts," because imprecise, will depend on how a court views a particular set of facts. It may also depend on whether it perceives that there is a forum interest in providing a forum plaintiff with a local court, or in declining to entertain a non-forum plaintiff's claim (see also 3.7.2). To return to the earlier contract example, sufficient local minimum contacts may be found to exist if the contract was concluded in the forum (perhaps only negotiated there but finalized elsewhere); it was to be performed in the forum; financing for it was obtained in the forum; or payment was to run through a local account. In contrast, only the contract's place of performance would justify the exercise of specific jurisdiction under the narrower EU law. For more on "relatedness," see 3.3.3.

3.3.2 "Stream of commerce" jurisdiction

Many sales of goods are not made by the producer/manufacturer directly to the ultimate user/buyer, but the goods reach the latter through a distribution system. This is, of course, particularly true of consumer transactions. Is there specific (claim-related) jurisdiction wherever the product ultimately injures the end-purchaser or even a third party? Does the maker of the product expose itself to such jurisdiction by putting its product into the "stream of commerce"?

EU law focusses on the "place where the harmful event occurred or may occur," without inquiring how the product got there or even whether the producer could foresee or expect its product to reach that place; whether the defendant maintained "minimum contacts" with the forum is not an issue. To afford the defendant some protection against unfair surprise, EU law then limits the instances in which the forum of the injury may apply its own law to the claim. Instead, it must be a law that the producer could foresee as possibly applicable (see 4.3.1.1.2).

Despite the theoretically far more extensive scope of "minimum contacts" under American law (see 3.3.1), the defendant must have brought these contacts about itself, rather than through a third party. A 2011 plurality decision of the United States Supreme Court (and therefore not fully conclusive for lack of a definite holding)[3] declined to uphold a state court's exercise of specific jurisdiction in tort when a foreign manufacturer's machine, marketed in the United States, but not sold by the manufacturer itself into the forum state, caused injury in that state. Contact with the

---

[3] *J. McIntyre Machinery, Ltd. v. Nicastro*, 564 U.S. 873 (2011). A "plurality decision" is one in which a majority of judges agree on the result but differ with respect to the reasons for their vote. There is therefore no "majority opinion," and no one view constitutes a "holding" that would be a precedent for future cases.

state had not been established by the defendant directly, so there was no "stream of commerce" jurisdiction, said the Court's plurality. As a result, and as the forceful dissent noted, a foreign company that intends to market its goods in the United States but introduces its product through an independent distributor into a particular state can shield itself against being subject to jurisdiction in that state for product liability.

Since 2011, a number of lower court decisions have upheld specific jurisdiction when the product's maker knew where its products would end up, perhaps through a shared marketing purpose with the intermediate party that introduced the product into the forum state. A response from the United States Supreme Court to this interpretation of its very restrictive 2011 decision must await a future case (but see 3.3.3, immediately following).

3.3.3   "Relatedness" versus "arising out of" in American law

While the United States Supreme Court's case law limited general jurisdiction of business enterprises to states in which they were "at home" (see 3.2.2), the *J. McIntyre* decision[4] seemed to require a causal relationship between the defendant's action (such as introducing the product into the forum state) and the claim (such as injury in the forum state). Both case-law developments made the exercise of jurisdiction over business enterprises more difficult.

The United States Supreme Court's 2021 decision in *Ford v. Eighth Judicial District Court of Montana*[5] may bring about a change. In this decision the Court upheld jurisdiction over the Ford Motor Company in a damage action for death caused by a defective Ford motorcar, bought outside the forum state and brought into it by the decedent herself. The defendant did nationwide business, maintained sales and service establishments itself or with contract parties in the state, and advertised and sold the very same model car in the state. Even though there was no causal relationship between the company's conduct and the death giving rise to the claim, the latter was sufficiently "related" to the company's in-state business to justify the exercise of specific jurisdiction. Such exercise, given the company's business activity, was not "unfair" and it also sup-

---

[4]   Ibid.
[5]   141 S.Ct. 1017 (2021).

ported the state's interest in providing a forum for claims arising in it and brought by or on behalf of local residents.

The *Ford* decision perhaps does not change *J. McIntyre* (see 3.3.2), because the defendant in the latter did not engage in extensive trade with same products in the forum state. Nor does it answer whether and when "stream of commerce" jurisdiction may be exercised. What it does do, to some extent, is to soften the effect of the restriction on general jurisdiction over business enterprises by somewhat expanding specific jurisdiction – "relatedness" suffices, "arising out of" is not required. What and how much contact is required for "relatedness" remains an open question: hardly any enterprise will have the same nationwide involvement in most or all states as had the Ford Motor Company.

3.3.4   Weaker party protection in contract in the EU

The specific and narrow rules on specific jurisdiction in EU law (see 3.3.1) might disadvantage some weaker parties in contract cases (for tort, see 3.3.2) – typically, consumers, employees, and insureds – who do not meet these strict requirements and would need to sue the defendant at the latter's domicile (general jurisdiction). EU law addresses this problem by allowing the weaker party to sue at home under certain conditions. For instance, in contract, when the defendant pursues commercial or professional activities in a Member State that is the plaintiff's domicile, or "directs activities to" that state, or to several states including that state, the defendant must come to the plaintiff, rather than the other way around (as is the ordinary rule). The basis is a type of "minimum contacts" approach. A causal relationship, even only "relatedness" in the sense discussed in 3.3.3, is not expressly required but will factually usually be the case. To reinforce this weaker party orientation, these provisions proscribe forum-selection clauses that would circumvent the protection of these jurisdictional rules.

3.3.5   Weaker party protection in American law

In the United States today, weaker party protection is found mainly in provisions of substantive law relative to product liability in tort, and in some minimal regulation of warranties in contract law. The concept of a "class action" (see further 3.4) permits parties with relatively small claims of the same kind to sue their common defendant as a class, perhaps at the latter's domicile, thus without themselves having to leave their home. A 2005 federal law limited access to the class action format.[6]

Possibly more important (and as mentioned at 2.3.2) is the fact that, in many cases, private dispute resolution has eliminated recourse to the courts altogether. General conditions incorporated in many consumer contracts require the consumer to submit any future dispute to private arbitration in lieu of litigation. Examples include bank account applications, airline or cruise tickets, hospital admission agreements, credit card agreements, mobile phone contracts, and End User License Agreements (EULAs) that come with computer software. Many of these agreements also allow the service provider to change the terms of service unilaterally; the consumer is almost invariably deemed to have agreed to such a change after a waiting period for objections. And if the consumer does object, the agreement might terminate.

The result of these clauses is severe: no suit by the consumer, no jury trial, no class action, not even class arbitration. All this benefits the stronger party because it need not fear potentially high jury awards. The injured party might simply abandon its claim, as the inability to join with others may make submitting to individual arbitration prohibitively expensive. If arbitration is pursued, and the individual plaintiff faces corporate arbitration lawyers, the rate of success for the individual has been shown to be low. What is more, arbitration produces no binding precedent; indeed, the lack of published records prevents a consumer from finding out how similar claims were handled in the past. Nevertheless, the United States Supreme Court has upheld this practice (and thereby invalidated state laws attempting to limit required individual arbitration) in deference to the federal policy in favor of arbitration, as expressed in the Federal Arbitration Act.[7] As a result, American law thus largely lacks weaker party protection on the jurisdictional level in consumer transactions (for tort, see 3.3.2).

A group of attorneys provided help with a non-statutory novelty: Through social media they encouraged persons with like claims to file individual

---

[6]   Class Action Fairness Act of 2005, 28 U.S.C. §§ 1332(d), 1453, 1711–15.
[7]   *AT&T Mobility LLC v. Concepcion*, 563 U.S. 333 (2011); *DIRECTV, Inc. v. Imburgia*, 577 (U.S.), 136 S.Ct. 463 (2015). See also *Viking River Cruises v. Moriana*, (U.S.), 142 S.Ct. 1906 (2022).

arbitration claims through them. When this campaign resulted in thousands of requests for arbitration against the same company, the latter dropped its individual arbitration requirement clause in its contracts, thereby enabling claimants to litigate, including in class actions (see 3.4). Obviously, this kind of action cannot work if and where lawyers may not encourage such actions and offer their services to that end, nor is it likely to be used against smaller enterprises when the rewards would be less. The fact therefore remains that there is less weaker party protection in the United States than, for instance, in Europe.

3.4   Class actions

Claims are often so small that the expense of litigation may deter injured parties from pursuing them. The "class action," also "collective action," permits parties to bundle their claims if, in American terminology, these claims present "common questions of law and fact." The cost of litigation for the individual class member becomes minimal, or at least affordable, and class members share the winnings. This form of action is also attractive to attorneys, especially in countries like the United States, where they may charge contingent fees on a percentage basis. Some class actions have received wide publicity, especially when they resulted in very high recoveries, as is not uncommon in the United States. The size of the awards also results from the fact that class actions often seek and obtain punitive damages in addition to compensation. To curb excesses somewhat, the United States Supreme Court has held that punitive damages may only punish conduct in the particular state, and not nationwide, and that they should "ordinarily" not exceed compensatory damages by more than a single or low double-digit multiplier.[8]

Class actions are by no means unique to the United States, although preconditions and procedures of course vary from country to country. Over the years, collective action legislation has been passed in Asian countries (for instance, India, Japan, Korea, and Singapore), in Canada, and in Europe (France, Italy, the Netherlands, and the United Kingdom). Only Switzerland has no such legislation, and collective action is limited in Germany mainly to injunctive relief on behalf of consumers against

---

[8]   *State Farm Mut. Auto Ins. Co. v. Campbell*, 538 U.S. 408 (2003).

certain anticompetitive practices, like price fixing. Some countries do not permit direct class actions, but for practical purposes do provide avenues for collective relief (for instance, Austria, where claims are assigned to a central body, and Japan, where a "qualified consumer organization" must first be certified).

Countries also differ (in detail) as to who is bound by a decision in a class action: Do they include only persons who affirmatively agreed to participate ("opt in"), or everyone who meets the criteria for membership in the class and who did not exercise the right to "opt out" (and to sue individually)? In the United States, for instance, there is no right to opt out when litigation concerns a limited fund; only if everyone is bound can there be an equitable per capita distribution.

In the United States, many class actions used to be brought in state courts. These courts (with their local juries) often made very high awards, although practices among the states differed, and forum shopping resulted. The Class Action Fairness Act of 2005 (see 3.3.5) limited the type of action that can be brought in a state court, assigning all others to the federal court system. The latter fact will result in larger classes, although finding commonality among a larger group of class members may prove difficult. In turn, without "common questions of law and fact," fewer class actions will be certified in the first place. Combined with the tendency to channel disputes to mandatory individual arbitration (described in 3.3.5), limited class action availability may lessen weaker party protection.

3.5   Piercing the corporate veil for jurisdiction

Corporations ("legal persons") are separate entities. By incorporating a business, its owners (shareholders) separate themselves from their creation. The incorporated business has limited liability. In some circumstances, the law of some countries permits the disregard of this separateness ("lifting the corporate veil"), most often to permit a closely held company to recover damages from a shareholder for acts (often fraud) that have caused the company losses. The loss then is not the company's; it can be visited on the shareholder. Such piercing of the corporate veil in the context of closely held corporations is a much-litigated issue in the

United States. It is used rarely in the United Kingdom and other countries (such as Germany).

The doctrine is relevant in the present context when a corporation (the "subsidiary") is owned wholly or in substantial part by another (the "parent company"), which is its controlling shareholder. Does common or controlling ownership make them "one company," so that a plaintiff, for instance, can reach the parent and its assets by suing the subsidiary? This could be done by viewing the subsidiary as the parent's agent. It could also be done by attributing the subsidiary's contacts with the forum to the parent (as in the agency approach, thus still considering both as separate entities), or by disregarding their legal separateness altogether. The last of these pierces the corporate veil by considering both companies a single enterprise (economic entity).

In all approaches, the underlying idea is that an out-of-state business engaged in intrastate business should not be able to insulate itself from the reach of forum state jurisdiction through incorporation of a local subsidiary. Piercing, if successful, subjects the parent to jurisdiction at the location of the subsidiary and also lets the successful plaintiff reach the assets of the parent. The enterprise theory has received much discussion in American legal literature, but the United States Supreme Court has not yet addressed the issue. The relatively few cases in which the parent was reached through the subsidiary stopped short of piercing and employed agency notions.[9]

Piercing for jurisdictional purposes is largely unknown in other countries. A provision in EU law, however, provides special protection to consumers, employees, and insured persons. For instance, a non-EU "party" that has a "branch, agency or establishment" in an EU Member State and has entered into a contract with an EU consumer is subject to jurisdiction in that state for "disputes arising out of the operation of the branch, agency or establishment" (Brussels Ia Regulation, Art. 17(2)). In the case of a branch, separateness of the units is not involved. "Agency" also involves no piercing, while "establishment" – a term left undefined – might.

---

[9]   See Peter Hay, "Piercing the Corporate Veil in American Procedural Law," in Boris Paal et al. (eds), *Deutsches, Europäisches und Vergleichendes Wirtschaftsrecht – Festschrift für Ebke* 337 (Munich, C.H. Beck Verlag, 2021).

3.6   Jurisdiction in domestic relations cases

3.6.1   Introduction

Litigation in family law (domestic relations) cases is different from litigation in most civil and commercial law matters. Personal (non-material) relationships are at issue, and often not all parties are before the court, for instance, in an ex parte divorce, and often in custody and maintenance cases. In addition, the subject of the dispute may be something other than the rights and obligations of the immediate parties, for instance, when the best interests of the child are the focus of a contest for custody.

Concepts of marriage may differ among legal systems, and that may have implications for the recognition of a marriage in a state other than the one in which it was concluded. For instance, will a polygamous marriage be recognized in a Western European country? What about a foreign marriage according to tribal law or custom, i.e., without any formality that might be required in the second (recognizing) state? Similarly, religious differences become important for the recognition of a foreign marriage or divorce. What if the foreign state's religious law permits marriage between parties more closely related than permitted under the forum state's law on degrees of consanguinity? What if the foreign state's religious law permits some form of private divorce, like the *talaq* of Islamic law or the Jewish *get*?

These differences reflect the strong societal and religious interests of states and communities in ordering and regulating the domestic relationships of their citizens or inhabitants. A second (recognizing) state, often a new state of residence of the parties, similarly has societal interests underlying its law. Jurisdictional rules – just like rules or approaches with respect to the applicable substantive law – must seek to accommodate these interests, both private and public.

3.6.2   Marriage

Marriage usually raises no jurisdictional issues; the state where it is contracted establishes the preconditions (e.g., capacity) and procedures under its law. That law may refer to another law, for instance, that of a party's nationality, for issues such as capacity to marry. Still, it is the forum's law that establishes the rules and determinations necessary for a marriage in its state. Formalities also differ. Usually, however, a license, issued by a state authority, is required, for which compliance with the state's prerequisites, for instance as to capacity (e.g., legal age), is examined. The marriage is then concluded by a civil official, in many countries preceded or followed by a religious ceremony. In some countries (for instance, Greece, Italy, and the United States), a religious ceremony, performed by an ordained cleric of the particular religion, may substitute for a civil ceremony. In the United States, some religious organizations (that are not part of one the main religions) may "ordain" a private party to be a "minister" to conclude a particular, specified marriage, provided that the parties obtained a state license. On the other hand, some jurisdictions may provide particularly strict forms of marriage, such as the "covenant marriage" in three American states, which is more difficult to dissolve than the more usual civil marriage. Special religious elements may also be part of marriage, such as the *ketubah*, the marriage contract of Jewish religious marriages, or the *mahr* of Islamic marriage contracts, the future husband's gift or promise of a gift to his future wife.

Same-sex marriage was very controversial in the United States some years back. Federal law used to leave it to the individual states to permit or to forbid same-sex marriages – and to refuse recognition to ones concluded out-of-state. The United States Supreme Court ultimately held that federal statute to be unconstitutional and same-sex marriage is now available throughout the United States.[10] Elsewhere, many countries (for instance, Canada, and countries in Europe and South America) now permit such marriages, while others (for instance, Israel and Switzerland) provide for the registration of same-sex partnerships with rights and obligations similar to (or even the same as) in a marriage, without, however, equating the two entirely. In contrast, a large number of countries continue not to provide for any kind of formalized same-sex relationship (for instance, Poland and Russia), or to forbid these outright as part of their criminal laws (for instance, Nigeria).

---

[10]   *Obergefell v. Hodges*, 576 (U.S.), 135 S.Ct. 2584, 192 L.Ed. 2d 609 (2015). The 2022 Protection for Marriage Act now prohibits denial of recognition of a marriage celebrated in an American State on the grounds of sex, race, ethnicity, or national origin. Relevant for foreign county marriages is the new conflicts rule that the law of place of celebration determines the validity of a marriage, 28 U.S.C.A. § 1738C.

Private marriage – that is, marriage as a result of private contract – has ancient origins and can still be validly concluded in a number of countries. It may take the form of a "self-uniting" ceremony by the parties in front of witnesses, or may be the informal cohabitation of a man and woman who act and consider themselves as husband and wife. The latter form of marriage has its origin in countries with a common law background. In addition to the spouses' perception of themselves as "married," a "common-law marriage" also required acceptance and recognition of the parties' marital state by the community. In the United States, several states still permit common law marriages, while others have abolished this form of marriage. Nonetheless, even in the latter states, such a marriage validly entered elsewhere will be recognized as valid. This result derives from the general principle – equally observed with regard to different forms of civil religious marriages – that the *lex celebrationis* (the law of the state in which the marriage was concluded) applies to the issue of its validity. An exception applies when the foreign marriage violates the public policy of the second state: This may lead to the non-recognition of foreign same-sex marriages or legal unions in countries that still oppose these relationships, as did many states in the United States until 2015, and as a number of countries, for instance in Eastern Europe and the Middle East, still do today.

The validity, attributes, and consequences of a marriage or other form of legal union will therefore differ, depending on the state of celebration. These differences may then become an issue in a second state, for instance, in the context of the recognition of a marriage for such purposes as support, child custody, inheritance rights, and the like. For marital property rights, see 4.6.1.3.

3.6.3   Divorce

In the second half of the twentieth century, a great many countries that previously did not allow divorce introduced legislation making civil divorce possible, although with substantial differences in preconditions that must be satisfied. As a result, only the Philippines and the State of Vatican City today do not provide for civil divorce. In some societies, religious or customary forms of divorce take the place of civil divorce. In some Muslim countries, for instance, and of course with variations, *talaq* permits the husband to divorce the wife by simply making a traditional statement to that effect, while the wife would require the intervention of religious authorities to compel the husband to pronounce the *talaq* or to act in his stead. In general, countries with civil divorce, for instance the United Kingdom and the United States, will recognize religious divorces obtained by foreign domiciliaries if valid where obtained. However, the inequality between husband and wife in a divorce by *talaq* prompted at least one American court to refuse to recognize such a divorce. On the other hand, divorce by *talaq* gives Philippine husbands a way to divorce their wives when the country's civil law does not. Some Muslim countries are now abolishing divorce by *talaq* (for instance, India, Bangladesh, and Pakistan).

The Jewish letter of divorcement (*get*), delivered by the husband to the wife, is required for a Jewish couple to obtain a divorce under the auspices of the Israeli Rabbinical Court. A family court has civil divorce jurisdiction in Israel when one spouse is non-Jewish. Problems can arise when a Jewish husband divorces his Jewish wife in a civil proceeding in a country other than Israel but refuses to give her the *get*. Under the divorcing country's civil law, he is free to remarry, but under Jewish religious law, she is not. New York solved this problem by statute: A person seeking a civil divorce there must, as a precondition, remove all impediments to the remarriage of the other spouse.

In some countries, the parties may also divorce each other by themselves, that is in a non-judicial procedure. These are bilateral private divorces (as distinguished from the one-sided religious divorces mentioned above). Are they entitled to recognition elsewhere – for instance, are they a "divorce" within the meaning of the Brussels II *bis* Regulation in the European Union? EU Attorney General Collins so advised, whenever the private divorce is recognized by public authority in the EU country where the parties declared it.[11]

Most countries with legislation for judicial civil divorce provide for no-fault divorce, perhaps – like India – also providing for divorce by "mutual consent," while some continue to require that the respondent

---

[11]   Opinion of Attorney General Collins in Case C-646/20, referred to it by the German Bundesgerichtshof, concerning a private divorce in Italy registered and documented by the Italian Registrar in accordance with Italian law. ECJ Doc. 62020CC0646 (May 5, 2022). This interpretation will, of course, also apply to the successor Brussels II *ter* Regulation.

spouse be at fault (enumerating grounds constituting fault). General, no-fault preconditions usually include waiting periods of various lengths (from a number of months up to two years) after the spouses have separated or the petitioner has moved to the forum state. Their purpose may be to assure that the marriage has indeed broken down, or also to protect the forum state from becoming a "divorce mill." Some jurisdictions, however, have done the latter by choice (for instance, Haiti and the Dominican Republic, and the state of Nevada in the United States). Some jurisdictions (for instance, the EU) provide for waiting periods of different lengths, depending on whether the forum was the habitual residence of both spouses, the petitioner was a habitual forum resident during the marriage, or the petitioner has now been habitually resident for the specified period (or for an even shorter period if also a forum citizen).

Often only one of the spouses is before the court, for instance, when abandoned by the other, or when a petitioner seeks an "ex parte" divorce in a state with a relatively short waiting period. An "ex parte" divorce enables a spouse to obtain a divorce in circumstances when it would be difficult to obtain personal jurisdiction over the other spouse. On the other hand, the absent spouse loses the status of "being married" without having participated. The fact that "fault" (on the part of the respondent/defendant) is no longer required justifies such unilateral action by the divorcing state: The petitioner's statement of the breakdown of the marriage would be enough in a bilateral divorce as well. The waiting periods, moreover, are intended to assure that the divorcing state has a connection to the petitioner and can assert a societal interest in his or her status. In the United States, the rule that the petitioner's domicile justifies the exercise of divorce jurisdiction derives from a legal fiction: Through his or her domicile in the forum state, the petitioner brings the marriage into the state and before the court. The latter is then acting upon the marriage, treating it as a thing (*res*); it is exercising *in rem* jurisdiction. For the resulting concept of "divisible divorce" in the United States, see 3.6.5.

3.6.4   Child custody

Divorce or legal separation is often accompanied by the need to decide who should have custody of the child or children of the household, or whether joint custody by the parties might be the appropriate solution.

Unhappily, custody proceedings can often be very contentious. The child can become the means by which the parties continue to express the animus they have toward each other. Indeed, the parties' fight over custody frequently continues after a custody decision has been rendered (or while a case is pending), with the unsuccessful party removing ("kidnapping") the child from the jurisdiction to try to obtain an award or modification in another state or country.

An early United States Supreme Court decision, never formally abandoned, referred to a parent's "right in" the child, consequently requiring a court to have personal, *in personam* jurisdiction over a parent before his or her "right" to the child could be terminated. Modern national legislation and international treaty practice rightly focus on the child and the child's best interest, and not on any right or entitlement of one of the parents. The EU's relevant law and the national law of some other countries, for instance Australia, reflect this orientation in framing the issue as the question of who should exercise "parental responsibility." This may even include persons who are not the child's parents.

Procedures and the form of the custody decision of course differ among countries. In most, a court (or a referee) renders a decision that encompasses both physical (residential) custody and decision-making power and rights with respect to the child's affairs. In both Japan and China, these are separate aspects of custody. In Japan, for instance, the person with physical custody (*kangoken*) requires the consent of the party with *shinken* (decision-making, legal custody) for changing the child's residence. Whatever the formal differences, the focus on the child – everywhere at the forefront – has direct importance for the question of jurisdiction to make the custody decision. It lies with the court (or other authority) of the place where the child physically is. American law and that governing the 27 Member States of the EU (Brussels IIa Regulation) are more express: The court of the child's "home state" has jurisdiction for both the original custody decision and any later decision to modify the custody arrangement (unless a new state has meanwhile become the child's "home state"). American law (by uniform legislation adopted by the individual states) defines "home state" as the state in which the child has resided for the preceding six months. European law achieves a similar result by requiring that the child has been "habitually resident" in the state in which a determination is sought.

In both of the foregoing examples, "residence" of the child means *legitimate* residence, that is, residence not in violation of a custody decree of another court that had proper jurisdiction. The requirement of legitimate residence is designed to provide a basis for relief in cases of interstate or international child abduction by a disappointed parent seeking to overturn the original court's decision.

What if a child is *not* a legitimate resident when a custody decision is sought? The Convention on the Civil Aspects of International Child Abduction[12] of the Hague Conference on Private International Law, in force in 102 countries (in 2022), provides for the return of the child to the state from where he or she was taken, and to do so without itself addressing the merits of the custody decision. Any modification is up to the court that issued the custody decision. Only exceptionally may the second court refuse to return the child, for instance, when return would expose the child to a dangerous or abusive environment. The United States has essentially similar legislation to deal with child abduction as among the individual American states, and the EU has built on the Hague Convention with additional provisions in its parental responsibility legislation.

The relief mechanism provided by the Convention has worked well in practice. The United States Supreme Court, as well as some courts elsewhere, has enlarged upon the Convention's protection by holding that "*ne exeat*" orders touch upon "rights of custody." If violated, they entitle a party to seek return of the child. "*Ne exeat*" orders are typically issued while a divorce and/or custody proceeding is pending. They prohibit removal of the child during the pendency of the case and thereby serve to preserve the court's jurisdiction.

3.6.5   Maintenance, child support, and the like

Upon divorce or separation of spouses, but also in other circumstances, national laws establish obligations for one person to support another. When does a court have jurisdiction to decree (or modify) such an obligation, especially in circumstances when the decree may need to be enforced in a country other than its own? The answer is easy, of course, when both parties are before the court, for instance, as in a bilateral divorce. The same

---

[12]   October 25, 1980, 1343 U.N.T.S. 89.

is true when the issue concerns the division of property upon divorce: The court can even affect foreign real property beyond its direct jurisdictional reach by personally obligating a party to convey to the other. But what if the divorce is *ex parte* (only the petitioner is before the court), or if a party (again without the other spouse present) seeks modification of an earlier support decree issued elsewhere?

In the United States, a marriage (the "status" of being married) is analogized to a thing (a *res*) so that a court can exercise *in rem* jurisdiction and grant a divorce when the status "is before it" through the petitioner and his or her close connection to the state, even when the other spouse is absent (see 3.6.3). Maintenance, whether for the divorced spouse or for the child of the parties, is a personal obligation and requires personal (*in personam*) jurisdiction over the (absent) debtor. The American concept is that of "divisible divorce" – the separate jurisdictional requirements for the status decision and the establishment of personal obligations. How is it possible to satisfy these jurisdictional requirements when the debtor possibly resides abroad? The Hague Conference on Private International Law's Convention on the International Recovery of Child Support of 2007,[13] in force in 45 countries (in 2022), including EU countries (except Denmark), and the United States, but not China, Japan, or Russia, provides a mechanism for establishing or enforcing a maintenance obligation for a child. It has much more limited application in cases of spousal support. Contracting states establish Central Authorities that transmit to each other requests for the initial establishment of a child support obligation or the enforcement of an obligation already decreed in the transmitting state against a person residing in the receiving state. The Central Authority of the receiving state then assists in locating the person, obtaining representation for the creditor in the transmitting state, and possibly even providing financial legal aid.

Australia maintains similar, but bilateral, reciprocal child support arrangements with a great many countries, including those of the EU and the United States, but not China, Russia, or Japan. In the United States, the Uniform Interstate Family Support Act[14] provides similar interstate coop-

---

[13]   Convention on the International Recovery of Child Support and Other Forms of Family Maintenance, Nov. 23, 2007, 47 I.L.M. 257.

[14]   Available at http://www.uniformlaws.org/, reprinted in 27 Fam. L.Q. 91 (1993).

eration (extending also to spousal support) for establishing and enforcing support obligations. The court that established the obligation thereafter has continuing jurisdiction to modify it, unless and until another court has acquired jurisdiction as a result of changes of residence of the parties.

The EU goes further. Its 2009 law on maintenance obligations provides for jurisdiction of the court at the *creditor's* habitual residence in the EU (without regard to the defendant's connection to the EU forum state). It also grants the court such jurisdiction when the maintenance claim is ancillary to its jurisdiction over a divorce or custody case pending before it. In situations when the law of a recognizing state requires that the debtor is or was personally subject to jurisdiction (as in the case of the United States: see 3.3), it is doubtful whether a decree based on such a far-reaching assertion of jurisdiction would be recognized.

3.6.6   Adoption

The adoption of a child or of an adult into the family has ancient origins but was unknown to the common law. Today, adoption is possible in common law countries, just as it is elsewhere. National laws differ with respect to the requirements (age of the adopter and of the person to be adopted, financial circumstances, and all other matters that bear upon "the best interest of the child," which is the universal standard under UN, Council of Europe, EU, and national and regional instruments). The emphasis today is on child adoption, although adult adoption remains socially important in Japan. In Germany, adult adoption remains possible if "morally justified," which is a requirement to assure that adoption is not used to circumvent immigration laws.

Jurisdiction ordinarily lies with a court or other authority where either the adopting party or the child is habitually resident. Of the greatest current interest and importance are intercountry adoptions, facilitated (and to some extent regulated) by the Hague Convention on Protection of Children and Cooperation in Respect of Intercountry Adoption.[15] It is in force in 104 countries (in 2022), but not in Japan, nor in the Russian Federation, which, however, has signed it. The Convention provides for cooperation between the central agencies of the adopter's and the child's states. These central agencies examine, respectively, the

---

[15]   May 29, 1993, 32 I.L.M. 1134.

suitability of the adopter and of the child proposed to be adopted, for which the Convention also provides criteria and guidelines. When both agencies agree and certify to each other that adoption is appropriate, the appropriate authority may decree it. Once decreed in conformity with the Convention, the adoption is entitled to recognition – as "a matter of law" – in all Convention countries. This is a very important aspect of the Convention because it eliminates the need for recognition proceedings under possibly varying national standards and criteria.

3.7   Dismissal for *lis pendens* or *forum non conveniens*

3.7.1   *Lis alibi pendens*

It can happen that litigation involving the same subject matter is pending ("*lis pendens*") in the courts of two different states or countries at the same time. This may indeed be quite intentional, to try to gain an advantage in the litigation. Assume, for instance, that a party files a claim against an insurance company that insists that the policy does not cover this particular loss. The insurance company, in an effort to seek protection, not only defends against the claim but brings an action in another court (that also has proper jurisdiction, as discussed earlier) for a declaratory judgment that the policy does not cover losses of this kind. The parties are engaged in a "race to judgment," as whoever wins first can plead its judgment as a bar to further proceedings in the other forum.

Parallel litigation is an uneconomical, additional burden on the court system. It is, of course, also expensive for the parties – and that very fact may encourage one party to engage in it to harass the other, perhaps to force a settlement. Civil law systems all provide relief against parallel litigation, generally by providing that the second court either dismiss or, as in the EU, abstain until the first court has established that it indeed has jurisdiction, and thereafter dismiss.

When statutes or procedural rules provide no explicit solution, court practice may provide relief. In the United States, federal courts will defer, by abstention, to the court where the action was "first filed." However, because a filing could be a tactical move designed to block a filing in another court, a refinement seeks to identify the first "effective" filing.

Obviously, things become uncertain again with such an open-ended test. However, two other procedural tools are available to common law courts (and also used in British, Canadian, and other common law courts), in contrast to courts in civil law systems: the anti-suit injunction and the dismissal for *forum non conveniens*.

Anti-suit injunctions seek to preserve the local court's jurisdiction as against parallel litigation elsewhere. If the local action were filed first, a foreign court's *lis alibi pendens* procedures would protect the local court, but if the foreign proceeding was first, an anti-suit injunction tries to override the foreign court's advantage. Such injunctions are of limited value, however. They can affect (bind) only the parties before the issuing court; the foreign court – indeed, no court – will allow another court to interfere with the exercise of its lawful jurisdiction by recognizing and considering itself bound by such an injunction. The party that has been enjoined can therefore proceed, albeit at its peril, because the issuing court may impose sanctions for ignoring its injunction. Dismissals for *forum non conveniens* protect the local court against being used when litigation really belongs elsewhere, as explained below.

3.7.2   *Forum non conveniens*

Originating in Scotland in the nineteenth century, the doctrine of *forum non conveniens* is now used by courts throughout the common law world, but not in civil law systems, as mentioned further below. The doctrine allows a court, in its discretion, to dismiss a case that more properly should be tried elsewhere. When is this the case? Usually, such a case will have little connection to the forum, even though the forum does have proper jurisdiction. Examples include when key facts occurred elsewhere, when witnesses and evidence are elsewhere and not in the forum, and when – as a result of the minimal local connection – there is no conceivable public interest to be advanced by having the litigation occur in the forum, especially when local courts are overburdened. Why would such a case be brought in this court in the first place? Because the plaintiff sought a perceived procedural or substantive law advantage in this court. In Lord Denning's famous dictum, litigants flock to the United States "as a moth is drawn to the light"[16] because they seek: a jury trial (that may result in

---

[16]   *Smith, Kline & French Labs., Ltd. v. Bloch*, [1983] 1 W.L.R. 730 (A.C.) at 733 (Eng.).

an award of high damages, possibly also punitive damages); much more far-reaching discovery of documents in the hands of the opposing party than they could get at home; possibly the application of more favorable local American law; and, if successful, easy execution into locally available assets of the defendant. In such circumstances, the defendant will seek to have the case tried elsewhere and will make a motion for dismissal on grounds of *forum non conveniens*.

The court will weigh public and private interests in deciding whether to grant the motion. In making its decision, it will give no weight to the possibility, or even the fact, that the plaintiff, if dismissed here, will have a less favorable law applied to his or her claim in the other court. However, the court protects the plaintiff in other ways (after all, the plaintiff did have a right to sue here): The court must make sure that an alternative forum is available, and will require that the defendant submit to that court's jurisdiction. In addition, it must require that the defendant waive all defenses that might arise between the time of dismissal here and the commencement of the case in the other court, for instance that the statute of limitations has run in the meantime.

Civil law countries do not use the doctrine of *forum non conveniens* for the reason that they do not consider courts to be free to decide not to exercise the jurisdiction that the legislature decreed them to have. Thus, in applying the jurisdictional law of the EU, the United Kingdom was not free to use the doctrine (valid under its domestic law) to dismiss a case in favor of a non-EU country when EU law provided for jurisdiction at the defendant's English domicile. However, EU legislation has now made an exception (but note, by legislation, not by discretionary court action): In child custody cases, a court may defer to another court that is better positioned to assess what custody determination would be in the best interest of the child.

3.7.2.1   Blocking statutes

Litigating in the United States is attractive to many foreign plaintiffs, as mentioned above. Dismissals are therefore also frequent. However, some Latin American countries would like their nationals to be able to proceed in the United States, and have adopted legislation designed to prevent such dismissals. These statutes provide that the courts of that country lose jurisdiction when suit has been initiated somewhere else. The "somewhere else" really targets the United States. Because of such a statute in the plaintiff's home country, an American court, when faced with a motion to dismiss for *forum non conveniens*, may now need to conclude that there is no alternative forum and therefore that it may not dismiss, lest doing so would deprive the plaintiff of access to justice. American courts have shown themselves to be uneasy about how to respond to these blocking statutes. Some have given them effect and have declined to dismiss the case, while others have ignored them, but left the door open for the plaintiff to return if indeed unable to sue elsewhere.

3.8   Jurisdiction over things – actions *in rem*

Previous discussion dealt with *personal* jurisdiction; the parties' dispute concerns their rights and obligations, for instance, to answer in damages for the breach of a contract or injuries caused in an accident. Two actions discussed above do not fit that description: child custody and divorce. In child custody cases, the focus is on the child. Parents (or others) do not have "rights" against each other to have custody, but may well have obligations toward the child (but not the other party) for support. In divorce, the parties are named "petitioner" and "respondent," but the proceeding goes ahead even if one does not appear or is otherwise not subject to the court's jurisdiction. In the custody cases, the court only needs to have proper jurisdiction over the child (i.e., to be the court of the child's "home state") to determine who should be responsible for his or her care and have physical custody. What does a court have in an ex parte divorce? How can it take away the absent spouse's being married?

American law provides a clear answer. Other legal systems also provide for ex parte divorce, but do not draw similar clear distinctions. In American law, as briefly discussed earlier (see 3.6.3), marriage is a "status" and is likened to a "thing." A court always has jurisdiction over "things" within its territorial jurisdiction, hence also over the "thing" called "marriage," if it is properly before it. It is the petitioner who brings the "thing" within the court's jurisdiction, provided that he or she fulfills the requirement of a sufficiently close connection to the divorcing state. The court then acts upon the "thing" (dissolving the marriage), but because the other party is absent, cannot do more, such as obligating the absent party to pay support.

The divorce example illustrates, in what seems like a borderline case, the distinction between *in personam* and *in rem* jurisdiction. The latter allows adjudication of matters about the thing, but not the personal rights and obligations of people since the latter requires *in personam* jurisdiction of all parties. Similarly, *in personam* jurisdiction may result in a judgment that a party should have a particular thing, but the court cannot give a property right to the thing to the winning party if the thing is elsewhere.

To illustrate: a house is in State A, and litigation is in State B, in which the plaintiff wishes to collect money that the defendant owes him, and for which the defendant has given him a mortgage on the house as security. With both parties before the State B court, that court can determine that the debt exists, and that the defendant must pay, but it cannot foreclose on the mortgage and give the plaintiff title to the house. To foreclose on the house and title to it, the successful plaintiff needs to get his State B judgment recognized and enforced in State A, because only the State A court has *in rem* jurisdiction over the house. In reverse, if the defendant home owner, with his creditor not before the court, gets the State A court to agree that he owes nothing and that the mortgage is canceled, the title to the house will now be clear and will be the owner's unencumbered property; the A court has power to do that. It could give the owner clear title to the local real property, but it does not have power to determine that the absent creditor has no claim. To establish that, the owner has to sue the creditor in a court with personal jurisdiction over the creditor.

3.9   Notice and service

To have jurisdiction over the opponent is not enough. As EU law puts it, "a [default] judgment shall not be recognized … if the defendant was not served with a document [commencing proceedings] … in sufficient time and in such a way as to enable him to arrange for his defense. …"[17] American law and other legal systems reach the same result: notions of "due process," in the sense of fundamental fairness, require an opportunity to defend, and for that, notice is required. All this can be reduced to the simple statement that – of course – jurisdiction is the primary require-

---

[17]   Council Regulation 1215/2012, Art. 34(2), 2012 O.J. L 351/1, 13 (EU) ("Brussels Ia" Regulation).

ment, but notice is required to perfect it. Conversely, notice alone cannot substitute for jurisdiction.

How does one give notice? Ordinarily, proper notice requires "service" on the other party, with the document initiating suit. National laws of legal systems differ on whether this requires actual personal service, whether substituted service (for instance, on a member of the household) or service by mail is permitted, and when – if none of the foregoing is possible, for instance, for lack of an address of the person to be served – service by publication, for instance, in national newspapers, is an acceptable substitute.

Some countries, notably France, but also Belgium, Luxembourg, and the Netherlands, permit service on a public official or through diplomatic channels. The official or diplomat then effects actual service on the defendant. This procedure, known as *remise au parquet*, has the disadvantage that time periods begin to run when service on the official has been effected, with the defendant therefore getting notice only later, possibly when time limits have already expired. The French Supreme Court (*Cour de cassation*) held in 2016[18] that time limits do not begin to run when service is made for transmission through diplomatic channels. The ruling does not address this problem when service is made on the designated court official. As a result of the provision of EU law quoted above, service by *remise au parquet* may not satisfy the EU law requirement of adequate notice.

Internationally, the Hague Convention on the Service Abroad of Documents,[19] in force in 80 countries in 2023, provides a mechanism to effect service in another country. Each contracting state designates a Central Authority, which receives documents from a local party and transmits them to its counterpart in another contracting state. The Central Authority in that state transmits them to the intended recipient and, of course, vice versa. The Convention also addresses such questions

---

18   Cour de cassation [Cass.] [supreme court for civil matters] 2e civ., June 2, 2016, No. 14-11.576, available at: https://www.legifrance.gouv.fr/affichJuriJudi.do?idTexte=JURITEXT000032635976 (accessed March 6, 2018).

19   Convention on the Service Abroad of Judicial and Extrajudicial Documents in Civil or Commercial Matters, Nov. 15, 1965, 20 U.S.T. 361, 658 U.N.T.S. 163.

as whether, in lieu of using its mechanism, a party may undertake to effect service directly, by international mail. The Convention leaves that up to the recipient's country, and some countries indeed do not allow service by mail.

As pointed out in connection with the Hague Convention on Civil Aspects of Child Abduction (see 3.6.4), international conventions can provide uniform rules only within limits because there is no mechanism for their uniform interpretation and application. National courts will quite naturally deal with conventions against the background of their own law. For instance, when an American plaintiff sought to sue the German carmaker Volkswagen in an American court,[20] it sought to comply with the service of documents requirement by serving the company's wholly owned American distributor. Did this comply with the Hague Convention on Service Abroad of Documents? The law of the particular American state considered the distributor the defendant's "agent" – thereby, in fact, piercing the corporate veil (see 3.5) – and permitted service on it. The United States Supreme Court affirmed: if the party served was the "agent" of the foreign defendant, then in-state service obviously was not service "abroad." Therefore, the Convention and its rules did not apply. As discussed earlier, piercing of the corporate veil is used more frequently in American practice than elsewhere. When international uniformity is the objective, special features of national law should not define treaty obligations and, in any case, notions of state law should not serve to define the reach of the obligation under federal treaty law. In the example given, the Convention arguably required service – through its mechanisms – on the defendant itself, and not on a party that a national law treated as the defendant's agent or alter ego.

3.10 Taking evidence abroad

In cross-border litigation, evidence (necessary documents or witnesses whose testimony is needed) will often be located in another state or country. How does one obtain that evidence? Here, common law (especially American) and civil law practices vary considerably, in large part as a result of how litigation is conducted in the first place.

---

[20]   *Volkswagenwerk Aktiengesellschaft v. Schlunk*, 486 U.S. 694 (1988).

In civil law countries, the court (the judge) gathers whatever evidence is required for an assessment of the parties' claims and defenses, evaluates that evidence (in other words, renders a decision on the facts), and then applies the law. The court thus performs the functions that, in a common law system, may be divided between judge and jury. The parties' lawyers assist the court in its fact-finding role by requesting that it order production of certain documents from the opposing or a third party or require someone's testimony. From this, it follows that the request must be specific, both as to what should be obtained and as to what this particular evidence or testimony is intended to support.

In common law countries, in contrast, and especially in the United States, the case is conducted by the parties (their lawyers). It is they who gather the evidence, generally before the trial, name the persons to be called as witnesses, and, if at a distant place, obtain their testimony beforehand. They present what they have gathered and the recorded or live witness testimony to a lay jury (unless the parties have waived jury trial, in which case the judge performs the fact-finding function as well). The jury decides what the facts are or were ("was the traffic light red or green when the party crossed the intersection?"), the court applies the law to the jury's verdict, and renders the decision.

In view of these differences in the conduct of the case, lawyers in a common law case must therefore have means to obtain evidence, primarily before trial. American law provides the most far-reaching means: A party can obtain a court order for "pretrial discovery," which can be non-specific and wide-ranging. Illustratively, such an order might require a party to produce all e-mail exchanges with certain other persons between March of two years ago and the date the order is received by the party. The only requirement is that the material sought to be produced is "nonprivileged … [and] relevant to any party's claim or defense and proportional to the needs of the case … Information [sought] need not be admissible in evidence to be discoverable."[21] Thus, while civil law orders

---

[21]   Federal Rule of Civil Procedure 26(b)(1). Pretrial discovery may also be used to obtain information for arbitration proceedings but not – so the U.S. Supreme Court held in 2022 – for overseas arbitration proceedings: *ZF Automotive US, Inc. v. Luxshare Ltd.*, 142 S.Ct. 2078 (2022).

seek *specified evidence*, American law permits a *search for evidence* or, as critics justifiably say, it permits a "fishing expedition."[22]

Other common law countries also provide means for the parties to obtain evidence. One example is search orders (formerly "Anton Piller" orders) in English practice. These orders have counterparts in Australia, New Zealand, and India. They order a party to permit entry to the premises to search for documents, especially to ensure their preservation. While obviously more far-reaching than a court-conducted search for identified evidence in civil law countries, these practices are still less invasive and less wide-ranging than American-type pretrial discovery.

To overcome the difficulties presented by these very different systems, courts formerly requested assistance from their counterparts in another country by way of letters of request (*letters rogatory*). The Hague Convention on the Taking of Evidence Abroad,[23] in force in 64 countries (in 2022), now institutionalizes this cooperative practice. National Central Authorities request and provide information by exchanging letters of request. An Inter-American Convention[24] parallels the Hague Convention. The latter specifies the form of such letters and the specificity required of the request. Its Article 23 permits countries to declare by reservation that they will not honor American-type pretrial discovery requests. All but four countries have made such reservations.

It is disputed whether the Convention substitutes (replaces) national law for the taking of evidence in another country or provides only an optional alternative. The United States Supreme Court takes the position that an American court may order American-type discovery if it has jurisdiction over the party whose evidence is in another country, although the trial court should consider using the Convention on the basis of "comity."

---

22   Germany amended its implementing statute of the Hague Evidence Convention in 2022 and now permits German courts to assist foreign courts in obtaining evidence in Germany, subject to several conditions. The latter include that the discovery request seek *specific* documents and that the documents requested are important and relevant for the outcome of the case. "Fishing expeditions" thus remain excluded.

23   Convention on the Taking of Evidence Abroad in Civil or Commercial Matters, Mar. 18, 1970, 23 U.S.T. 2555, 847 U.N.T.S. 231.

24   Inter-American Convention on the Taking of Evidence Abroad, Oct. 30, 1975, 1438 U.N.T.S. 390.

In response to the continued possibility that American-type discovery might be ordered, France enacted a blocking statute, forbidding the transmission of evidence abroad. Swiss law is to the same effect, and so are increasingly restrictive national privacy laws, under which information is privileged and may not be disclosed. Interestingly enough, American discovery rules may be used, within limits, to obtain evidence in the United States for use in litigation abroad. Whether evidence obtained in this fashion will be admitted by the foreign court is another question, given how evidence is sought, produced, and used quite differently in civil law litigation (as discussed above in this section).

PART II

The applicable law (choice of law)

4   What law applies?

4.1   Sources

4.1.1   Conventions

As mentioned earlier (see 1.2.1), choice-of-law rules (also "conflicts rules") may be contained in international conventions. This is the case, for instance, when a convention does not itself contain a substantive rule of law (such as "when may a contract be avoided?" in the International Sale of Goods Convention (CISG); see 4.2.1), but refers to a national law ("the law of the support creditor's habitual residence"). The Hague Conference on Private International Law has drafted a great number of conventions containing directly applicable rules (for instance, in the Service of Documents Convention: see 3.9) and choice-of-law rules. Member States of the Conference are free to sign, ratify, and then put into force conventions proposed by the Conference, or later to accede to one or another of them. The success of these conventions has been mixed; some have been signed and put into effect by a great many states, others by only a handful. The Service of Documents Convention is an example of the former; the Conventions on the Law Applicable to Agency,[1] and on the Administration of Estates of Deceased Persons[2] are examples of the latter, with four and three ratifications, respectively. Some conventions are signed by contracting states, but never put into effect. An example is the Trust Convention of 1985,[3] which the United States signed in 1988, but never ratified. The last example also demonstrates that it is a matter

---

[1]   Convention on the Law Applicable to Agency, Mar. 14, 1978, 16 I.L.M. 775.
[2]   Convention Concerning the International Administration of the Estates of Deceased Persons, Oct. 2, 1973, 11 I.L.M. 1277.
[3]   Convention on the Law Applicable to Trusts and on their Recognition, July 1, 1985, 23 I.L.M. 1389.

of national constitutional law when a convention becomes effective as domestic law (in the American example, not upon signing, but only upon consent to ratification by the United States Senate), and what rank it has domestically once effective – superior to national statutory law (e.g., Germany), or only equal to it, and thus vulnerable to change by subsequent inconsistent legislation (United States).

Hague Conventions, of course, attempt to reconcile worldwide differences in solutions and policy approaches, which explains both the difference in their success as well as the broad formulations of many rules that these conventions contain. The latter is demonstrated by the Choice of Court Convention (see 2.2.2). For the new Convention on Recognition of Judgments, see 5.3.1.

Bilateral conventions can be more specific, both with respect to norms of substantive law and to conflicts rules, because they deal with specifically identifiable differences in rules and policies of the partners that they are designed to reconcile. The many treaties to avoid double-taxation demonstrate the need to solve a concrete problem for business and individuals whose activities might expose them to taxation in both countries. The same is true of "Treaties of Friendship, Commerce, and Navigation," "Treaties of Commerce and Establishment," and the like. These may not be able to solve all substantive problems, but they may provide conflicts rules to that end, for instance, on the question of the recognition of a corporation's personality (place of incorporation or place of its seat).

Geography also plays a role. Neighboring countries, or those in defined regions, have traditionally resolved international problems and differences of substantive and conflicts law by treaty. This is so to a far greater extent than has been possible on a larger, let alone global, scale, which has been the aim of the Hague Conference. Examples are conventions produced by the MERCOSUR countries (Argentina, Brazil, Paraguay, Uruguay, Venezuela), and by the Inter-American Special Conference, as well as specialized conventions between and among Benelux countries, as well as Scandinavian countries.

4.1.2 Federal-like (supranational) law: the example of the EU

The EU evolved from the original European Common Market (1958), which later became the European Economic Community (EEC), and which is now based on the Treaty on European Union and the Treaty on the Functioning of the European Union (1993). In the early years, differences in national private substantive and conflicts laws of the Member States were reconciled by treaties, much like the regional treaties mentioned above. Examples are the early Brussels Convention on Jurisdiction and Judgment Recognition[4] and the Rome Convention on the Law Applicable to Contracts.[5] The organization's central authorities had rule- and decision-making power only with respect to issues relating to the "four freedoms" that were part of the common market (free movement of persons, freedom of establishment, freedom to render services, and free movement of capital). But even in the areas still regulated further by conventional treaties, the Member States went beyond the usual regional treaty by conferring jurisdiction on the organization's Court of Justice to review the acts of the institutions, and to make binding rulings on questions of interpretation and application regarding them referred to it by national courts of last resort.

With the revision of the constituting treaty to form the EU, the Union's institutions (Council, Commission, and Parliament) gained law-making power in areas formerly the subject of treaties. Thus, the Brussels Jurisdiction Convention became the "Brussels I Regulation" and the Rome Convention became the "Rome I Regulation." In the Union's terminology, "regulations" are like federal law in a federation: They are directly applicable throughout the Union and pre-empt (enjoy precedence over) prior or later national law that may be inconsistent. Again, the Court of Justice is the judicial body of review, much like a federal supreme court. Other regulations followed those mentioned: on divorce jurisdiction and recognition, child custody, applicable law in divorce, applicable law in tort, maintenance, jurisdiction, and applicable law regarding succession, and others. The original Brussels I and Brussels II (divorce and child custody jurisdiction and recognition) Regulations have since been promulgated in revised form. In all of these areas, EU jurisdiction and conflicts law replaces the national law of the Member States; in a few instances (civil jurisdiction, divorce and custody) only in their relation to each other, but in many others (conflicts law in contract,

---

[4]   1972 O.J. L 299/32.
[5]   Convention on the Law Applicable to Contractual Obligations, 1980 O.J. L 266/1.

tort, divorce, and succession) with respect to all other states, meaning that they are now of "universal application" in Member States' law.

4.1.3   National (domestic) law: in general

In the absence of international treaty rules that have been incorporated into national law or supranational, directly applicable regional law, as in the EU, national conflicts law applies. As discussed earlier, civil law and common law countries differ in their methodology. In civil law countries, conflicts law is typically statutory, overlaid by judicial interpretation and application. The judicial decision affects only the individual case but may possibly become a general formulation of a rule when consistently used by the particular country's highest court, reaching the level of *jurisprudence constante* (France) or *ständige Rechtsprechung* (Germany). Statutory rules may not help with future societal developments. Lest they become too rigid, they therefore need periodic amendment and adjustment, or escape clauses, that are built in from the beginning and to which courts can resort in cases that cannot be adequately resolved with the basic rule. "Escape" clauses are considered further below.

Statutory conflicts rules prevail throughout most of the civil law world, either in individual statutes or in comprehensive conflicts law codes. In European countries, the beginning of codification of conflicts rules coincided with the codification of substantive law (the *Code Napoléon* in France, followed by codifications in Austria, Italy, and Spain, and still later, the *Bürgerliche Gesetzbuch* in Germany). More recently, many countries have adopted new conflicts statutes or amended others. As one study showed, 94 countries codified some or most of their conflicts rules between 1962 and 2012.[6] Since then, other countries have followed. In 2022, a Working Group established by the French Ministry of Justice presented a proposal for the codification of French private international law.[7] Many of these have in common what now also characterizes the conflicts regulations of the EU: the use of alternative rules and escape clauses to provide some flexibility from the very beginning.

---

[6]   Symeon C. Symeonides, *Codifying Choice of Law around the World* 4–12 (Oxford: Oxford University Press, 2014).

[7]   See   Cuniberti,   eapil.org/2022/05/11/towards-a-french-code-of-private -international-law/ (last visited September 10, 2022).

In common law countries one finds some statutory conflicts law. Examples are, in the United States, the reference in the Federal Tort Claims Act[8] to the place of injury, or the English codification in 1995 of choice of law in tort (subsequently replaced by the EU's Rome II Regulation, retained after Brexit). To a large extent, however, choice of law in substantive areas of private law, such as in contract, tort, and inheritance, is judicially declared; it is case law. This does not mean that the traditional case law (before perhaps being superseded by conventions or regional federal-type law, such as in the EU) resulted in *ad hoc* decisions: The common law doctrine of the decisions of higher courts (precedent) binding lower courts – the doctrine of *stare decisis* (points of law "stay decided") – prevents lower courts from experimenting with new ideas on their own (but see the discussion of "characterization" at 4.3.4.1). Only the court that established the precedent can change it.

4.2   Party autonomy

All systems grant parties the freedom, though within differing limits, to stipulate what law shall apply to disputes arising from their transactions (for instance, their contracts) or from their relationships (for instance, tort claims arising in the context of a distributorship relationship created by contract). Whether non-contract related tort claims can be subject to a choice-of-law stipulation in advance of a tort is controversial. When party autonomy is addressed at all, it is usually restricted to stipulations entered into after the tort has occurred, however unlikely that is. The following therefore concentrates on such stipulations in contractual contexts.

4.2.1   Scope, limits, validity

By stipulating the applicable law, the parties' purpose is to achieve certainty, especially when, as in modern American conflicts law, it is often not predictable what choice-of-law decision the court will make in the absence of such an agreement. Since the parties wish the court to honor their selection, their agreement must be express. Many systems specifically so provide; in others it is simply assumed because it is

---

[8]   28 U.S.C.A. §§ 1346(b), 2671 et seq. (West, 2018).

really an obvious way to manifest agreement. But just as it is possible to infer agreement on the existence of a contract from circumstances and the parties' conduct, the question may arise whether the parties, who concluded a *choice-of-court* agreement in favor of a country, have – by implication – also made a choice of the law of that country. This would be in accord with the old maxim that he who chooses the court, chooses the law. This, however, may not be the majority view: To be effective as the *parties'* choice, the agreement must be *express*. However, it is still possible that the chosen court will apply its law – not because the parties chose it by implication, but because its approach to choice of law in the absence of a party stipulation leads it to forum law. For instance, a court might regard the choice-of-court clause as a *factor* in its determination of the law of the country with the "most significant relationship" to the transaction (see 4.3.3.3).

May the parties choose any law, or must it be related to the transaction? The American Uniform Commercial Code takes the narrow view: The chosen law must bear a relation to the transaction or there must be another good reason for it, otherwise forum law applies (although judicial practice has been more liberal). At the other end of the spectrum, some legal systems seem to impose no restrictions, for instance, EU law or the Hague Conference's Principles on Choice of Law in International Commercial Contracts:[9] If the parties so wished, they could stipulate a completely unrelated foreign law, even for an entirely domestic transaction. (Of course, they would be foolish to do this because they would saddle the court or themselves with the additional burden of having to determine the content of that foreign law if it ever came to litigation: see 4.8.2).

The EU's provisions on the parties' freedom to choose the applicable law are perhaps the most liberal so far, limited only in order to protect particular public and private interests, as discussed below. They contain no overarching restrictions, such as the stipulated law's relatedness to the transaction (which, therefore, could even be a purely domestic one). The Principles on Choice of Law in International Commercial Contracts, approved by the Hague Conference on Private International Law, closely track the EU model, though they are at once more restricted and broader.

---

[9]   March 19, 2015, available at: https://www.hcch.net/en/instruments/conventions/full-text/?cid=135 (accessed March 6, 2018).

They are more restricted in that they apply only to transactions between merchants (contracts concluded by persons in their trade or profession), thus paralleling the CISG of the UN Commission on International Trade Law (UNCITRAL),[10] which endorsed the Hague Principles. At the same time, the Principles are broader, in that they expressly endorse the parties' freedom to choose non-state law, for instance, principles and guidelines established by international organizations, merchants' associations, and the like. The Hague Principles have been adopted as statutory law by Paraguay.

Even seemingly unlimited private autonomy is subject to restrictions that inhere in the legal system that is asked to honor such a stipulation. One example of a restriction is that if the clause is the result of overreaching, most systems will not honor it, the same as they would not honor any other contract stipulation that came about in this way. Another example is if forum law contains a "mandatory norm" (see 4.7); no choice of another law will be upheld if it does not also contain such a mandatory norm. The EU Court of Justice so held when a stipulation of California law would have circumvented EU law providing for compensation to an agent, upon termination of the agency, for the goodwill created by the agent.[11] A third example, closely related, is the forum court's objection to the application of the chosen law when this would violate the forum's public policy, for instance, when the chosen law would honor gambling contracts, but forum law does not (see 5.5.5.2).

In addition, a limitation on party autonomy may be contained in other parts of the forum's legislation, also reflecting its public policy, as in the second and third examples in the preceding paragraph. These are typically statutory provisions designed to protect weaker parties. Rather than relying on the ordinary contract law defense of overreaching (the first example above), contracts with weaker parties may need to observe limitations specific to them. In the EU, for instance, a consumer may only be benefitted by an additional choice-of-law option but may not be deprived of home state law. Other similarly protected parties in the EU are employees and insureds.

---

10   United Nations Convention on Contracts for the International Sale of Goods, Apr. 10, 1980, 19 I.L.M. 668, 1489 U.N.T.S. 3.
11   Case C-381/98, *Ingmar GB v. Eaton Leonard Technologies*, 2000 E.C.R. I-9305.

The foregoing also answers the question of what law applies to the choice-of-law clause itself. In the first place, it is primarily forum law: The forum court is asked not to determine the applicable law on the basis of its conflicts law, but instead to do what the parties want. It will make that decision on the basis of its own perspective. At the same time, since the parties chose the other law, the validity of the clause also needs to be examined under the law chosen to apply to it (as part of the contract that is so subjected to that law). There are thus two hurdles: the initial one to get the forum to use the foreign law, and the second one to examine the clause under the chosen law. The Rome I Regulation on contracts makes special provision (see 4.3.1.1.1).

One further problem remains: What if the forum and the foreign law consider the choice-of-law clause to be valid, but the substantive parts of the contract are invalid under the chosen law? If the clause is seen as an integral part of the contract, the conclusion would then need to be, contrary to the earlier assumption, that the clause is invalid as well. The forum is then left without a choice by the parties and determines the applicable law under its conflicts rules. If, on the other hand, the choice-of-law clause is seen as separate from the contract's substantive provisions – as a contract of its own, as it were – then the choice would remain effective, but the contract itself would fail. Regarding the clause as separate from the contract's substantive provisions is the prevailing view. The result – that the contract then fails – is something the losing party has to bear: The parties should have foreseen such a possibility and made a different choice. Another view is that such a result is unfair because the assumption must be that the parties acted in good faith and indeed had intended to enter into a binding agreement. To enable them to achieve that goal, this view would assume that their choice of an invalidating law was a mistake, that the choice should therefore be disregarded, and that the forum's conflicts law should determine the applicable law.

4.2.2   Unusual cases: partial choice of law, "floating clauses"

Previous discussion assumed that the parties submitted their agreement to the application of a single law. May they submit only a part of their contract (or several parts) to another law (or several), leaving the remainder to be governed by the law applicable under the forum's conflicts rules? In theory, why not? If one endorses the idea of party autonomy in the first place, then all that has been added is the need to examine each choice individually for its validity, as discussed above. The result then is a contract, different parts of which are governed by different laws. Such a result is not unknown to American law, in which choice-of-law approaches generally provide for the determination of the applicable law to "each issue" of the contract. The contract is split into issue parts (*dépeçage*: see 4.3.4.2). European law, with exceptions (see 4.3.4.2), does not split a case. It is perhaps for this reason (as well as the increased burden on courts and parties to deal with multiple applicable laws) that the EU's provision, permitting a partial choice of law, is construed as permitting only one part to be governed by a different law from that otherwise applicable. In contrast, the Hague Principles (see 4.2.1) expressly provide states wishing to adopt them with an option: either a (single) partial choice, as under EU law, or a choice of different laws to different parts of the contract (Art. 2(b)).

A party, understandably, may seek to stipulate the application of its own law. When like interests of both parties understandably conflict, they may choose a third – neutral – law, just as they might choose a third, neutral court. They might also employ a "floating clause," whereby, for instance, they choose the defendant's law. Since it is not known who will sue whom in advance, the issue of which law applies is thus undetermined – it "floats" – until litigation. (Such a clause can, of course, be combined with a floating choice-of-court clause, for instance, the plaintiff's court, to which the defendant submits but which then applies the defendant's law.) An early objection to floating choice-of-law clauses was that there was no way, for lack of a definite applicable law, to evaluate the validity of a contract. That is, of course, true, but also not particularly relevant: It is necessary to deal with the validity of the contract (and of the parties' choice of law) only at the time of litigation, and at that point, the parties' choice has become definite.

4.3   How to determine the applicable law in the absence of a party choice: by rule or case-specific approach? The examples of contract and tort conflicts law

4.3.1   Civil law

As already mentioned, civil law countries deal with conflicts law by statute or code, that is, by preformulated specific rules. These may be amended as social circumstances change or, as in modern statutes, may themselves include provisions giving courts flexibility to adapt the rule, or even to depart from it. The extent of the flexibility that civil law rules permit somewhat resembles the modern American approach to choice of law, but is indeed much more principled and limited.

4.3.1.1 Example: EU conflicts law in contract and tort

Earlier discussion referred to the EU's "Rome I" and "Rome II" Regulations on choice of law in contract and in tort, respectively, in the meantime followed by such regulations on conflicts law in other areas. They represent modern approaches to choice of law, combining both the stability of the rule orientation of traditional law with the flexibility needed to arrive at accommodations according to circumstances. In contrast to the Brussels Ia and II*ter* Regulation, which apply only among Member States, these Regulations are of "universal application," in that the applicable law they designate may be that of any country, not just a Member State. In this way, these Regulations replace a Member State's conflicts law with regard to all subjects covered by them.

4.3.1.1.1 Contracts: Rome I

This Regulation deals with the law applicable to contractual obligations and is also of "universal application." As mentioned earlier, it begins with one of the broadest provisions on party autonomy anywhere. On its face, the parties may choose any law, except that they may not evade rules of forum law if nothing is related to the state of the chosen law. The exception, one might add, is really irrelevant, as the general public policy exception would take care of any "evasion." However, as mentioned above, there are rules in other provisions that effectively place limits on the parties' freedom (see 3.2.1 and 4.7).

The Regulation's general provision establishes rules for the law applicable to eight specific contracts, including for two very important categories of cases: the sale of goods (seller's habitual residence) and the rendition of services (provider's habitual residence). For contracts not covered, the Regulation retains the cumbersome and somewhat unfortunate provision of the predecessor Brussels Convention, where it was a principal rule: The applicable law is that of the state where the party who "is to render the characteristic performance" under the contract has his or her habitual residence. Thus, the forum's conflicts rules need first to find what law seems to apply to the contract and consult it to determine who is to render the characteristic performance. It might have been better to skip this cumbersome provision and to proceed directly to the two escape clauses, with which the provision concludes. The first, and they are in order of priority, calls for the application of the law of such other country that is "more closely" related to the contract. If there is none, then the law of the "most closely connected" non-specific state applies.

Special provisions protect weaker parties, as mentioned earlier. Thus, a consumer gets home law if the selling merchant "directs his activities" toward the consumer's state or to a geographic area of which that state is part (for instance, possibly either France, Belgium, or Luxembourg when the defendant did its internet business activities in the French language). Recall that this parallels the Brussels Ia rule on specific jurisdiction. Similarly, special rules protect employees and insureds. These provisions also put limits on party autonomy, by allowing only the choice of a law more advantageous for the weaker party.

Similarly limiting is the provision that the forum's "overriding mandatory norms" take precedence. They are an expression of legislative or case-law public policy, and not subject to displacement either by a party stipulation or by an otherwise applicable law. An example of such a norm's displacement of a party choice was given earlier (see 4.2.1). An interesting addition, not generally addressed in the conflicts systems of other states, is the issue of another state's mandatory norms. In a departure from the predecessor Rome Convention, which made no provision for this issue, Rome I provides that a court "may" consider the mandatory norm of the state where the contract is to be performed when the law of that state would make performance unlawful. Albeit very limited in scope and only discretionary, this is, of course, a most sensible provision: Application of a law in violation of such a norm might result in non-recognition of a judgment that the forum might render. Such a result might then lead to other claims and further litigation (for instance, for unjust enrichment for payment already received). Future trouble can thus be avoided by considering that particular other state's mandatory norms.

Finally, the question of whether there was consent to enter into a contract and whether the contract is otherwise valid is to be determined by applying the law of the state whose law would apply if the contract were (hypothetically) valid. As a general provision, this rule then also applies to the validity of choice-of-law clauses (see 4.2.1). Again, however, and always to be kept in mind, this rule can also be overcome by an overriding mandatory norm of the forum or by the forum's rejection of the result of the inquiry on the ground of the forum's public policy.

4.3.1.1.2 Torts and other non-contractual relationships: Rome II

Current American tort conflicts law either focusses on the forum or is freewheeling (which may lead to the same result: see 4.3.3.3, 6.3). In contrast, the EU's Rome II Regulation has a general tort provision. Additional provisions address special problems. These include product liability and liability for obligations imposed by law, rather than by contract, namely, for *negotiorum gestio* (agency without mandate), unjust enrichment, and *culpa in contrahendo* (pre-contractual liability).

The general provision refers first to the law of the place of injury. This clarifies the question whether it should be the law of conduct or of injury that is "the tort." It will be recalled that the EU Court of Justice interprets the Brussels Ia Regulation to provide for specific jurisdiction in either state. For applicable law, however, Rome I refers to the place of injury and expressly excludes both the place of conduct and the place where consequential injury may have been suffered. In this respect, the EU rule did not follow the former German approach, which gave the victim the choice of the more favorable law (*Günstigkeitsprinzip*) and which the current proposal for an American Restatement (Third) of Conflict of Laws picks up again (see 1.3.4, 1.3.5.1).

As a specific exception to the general rule, and other factors absent, the applicable law in tort law is that of the plaintiff's and defendant's common habitual residence. Today, this is also the rule in American law. The rule recognizes that the fortuitous place of the tort is less important than the common habitual residence of the parties: that state's law is part of their general expectation (the fortuitous tort quite apart). The state of residence also bears any socio-economic consequences of the injury, and, in the case of traffic accidents, is most likely the state in which an insurer provided coverage.

The law of the place of conduct, though not part of the general rule, is not always irrelevant. That state obviously has a regulatory concern that persons entering the state should be bound to respect. A special provision in the Regulation addresses this issue in the case of traffic accidents. The court entertaining the case and perhaps applying the law of the parties' common habitual domicile, which may be different from the place of injury, is directed to have regard for the rules of the road of the state of the accident.

Similarly, a special provision deals with product liability. In these cases, the undifferentiated application of the general place-of-injury rule can impose liability on the defendant in cases in which it could not foresee this. These are the cases of a product reaching the consumer in the "stream of commerce" – that is, through one or several intermediaries in the chain of distribution – which the manufacturer could not foresee. It will be recalled that the United States Supreme Court solves this problem by limiting the exercise of specific jurisdiction to cases in which the product that caused the injury was introduced by the defendant into, or was closely related to the defendant's conduct in, the forum state (see 3.3.1). That is, of course, an incomplete solution: If the defendant is not subject to jurisdiction in the United States, it can still be sued at home: if that state follows a place-of-injury rule, the defendant will still be subjected to unforeseen liability.

The EU solution makes more sense: Brussels Ia provides for specific jurisdiction in consumer contract cases in courts of the state of the plaintiff's habitual residence if the defendant "directed activities toward" that state (or a geographical area of which the state is a part), as discussed above in connection with Rome I. For product liability (tort), there is jurisdiction where injury occurred. The latter exercise of jurisdiction is wider than under United States law. But Rome II guards against the problem that the American solution leaves unaddressed: Its rule provides that the applicable law is not necessarily that of the state of injury but is a law that was in some way foreseeable by the defendant. The rule specifies how foreseeability is to be determined. The United States Supreme Court can provide a similar solution: It has authority under the United States Constitution to define the permissible reach of individual states' exercise of jurisdiction, as well as to establish limits for the application of forum law, but it lacks affirmative authority to prescribe particular rules on applicable law. In a recent decision it somewhat expanded the permissible exercise of specific jurisdiction (see 3.3.1), thereby benefitting the local (injured) plaintiff. The *Günstigkeitsprinzip* (above, this subsection) gives a plaintiff the opportunity to receive more than what his or her home law would provide as compensation by opting for the defendant's own stricter home law, thereby punishing the defendant for its conduct.

Excluding delicts, a number of obligations are imposed by law, rather than assumed by a party by contract, as already mentioned above. Legal systems differ on how to label, or characterize, these obligations. Agency without mandate and pre-contractual liability obviously lack a contractual basis. Unjust enrichment may or may not lack one. For instance, it may be a claim that is part of the winding-up of a contract that has gone awry. Except for pre-contractual liability (often treated as a business tort in common law countries), civil law countries often treat unjust enrichment and *negotiorum gestio* as part of contract. However, as mentioned, the EU Court of Justice, when called upon to define "contract" for purposes of specific jurisdiction under the Brussels Ia Regulation, and wanting to keep that jurisdiction narrow, held that a contractual obligation must be consensual.[12] None of the three obligations mentioned is undertaken consensually, but each is imposed by law as the consequence of a party's conduct. Following the EU Court's precedent, Rome II therefore deals with these claims as part of its overall treatment of "non-contractual liability." However, since these claims often arise in a contractual *context*, the appropriate rules instruct usage of the law applicable to that contract for such cases.

The award and amount of damages are also governed by the law applicable to the tort obligation. The EU focus is on compensation. American-type punitive damages are not part of EU national laws (nor with a limited exception in England): punishment is part of the criminal justice system (with its own particular defendant-protective rules), not part of private civil litigation. A subsequent section (5.5.5.1) addresses the question of how EU Member States deal with the recognition of non-EU judgments that may award punitive damages.

Again, although damages are part of the law applicable to the tort, this may inure to the detriment of a plaintiff living in a high-cost state, but injured in a low-cost one. The introductory recitals to Rome II contain a statement encouraging a court, in assessing damages, to bear in mind

---

[12]   Case C-344/00, *Fonderie Officine Meccaniche Tacconi SpA v. Heinrich Wagner Sinto Maschinenfabrik GmbH*, 2002 E.C.R. I-7357.

post-injury medical and other expenses that the injured party may incur in his or her home state.

Another exception relates to environmental damage claims. In contrast to the early German *Günstigkeitsprinzip*, discussed earlier, Rome II generally settles for the place of injury. However, its Article 7 retains the alternative reference for "damage sustained by persons or property as a result of [environmental] damage." Recital 25 of the Introductory Recitals (see next paragraph) points out that this provision expresses the policy that "the polluter pays," and that this policy "fully justifies … discriminating in favor of the person sustaining the damage." This policy benefits the victim in a state making low damage awards. But will it make that state adopt tighter standards and regulations and itself provide for higher awards? The defendant in a higher award-level state pays for his or her conduct in that state as a result of the lower standards of the victim's state.

It should be noted in this connection that all of these Regulations contain introductory recitals, which are sometimes very extensive. Recital 25 in the environmental damage context (above) is an example. These recitals are not part of the law, as such, but are valuable indications of the legislative intent behind the statutory law that follows. Therefore a court should follow them when applying a provision such as the one relating to damages in the above example, even though the general provision describing the reach of the Regulation includes damages as being covered and thus usually governed, by the place-of-injury rule. Introductory recitals are therefore an important source for legislative history and intent and should always be consulted.

Like Rome I, Rome II also contains an escape clause, allowing the court to apply the law that is "more closely" connected to the tort, rather than the rule otherwise provided by the Regulation. Since the parties often are not strangers, but may have maintained some kind of relationship, the escape clause continues by providing that the law applicable to such a relationship should apply if the tort is connected to it. This parallels the provisions noted above, in connection with unjust enrichment and the other two non-contractual obligations, providing that in the case of an underlying contractual relationship, the law applicable to it should also apply to this obligation. Both references to the law applicable to a related relationship avoid splitting claims arising from a single relationship into different claims – one in tort, the other possibly in contract. This is very much in the civil law tradition of treating a relationship as a whole in all of its aspects, rather than splitting it into different issues, as modern American law does (discussed at 4.3.4.2).

4.3.2   Rule orientation in the common law

Classic civil and common law conflicts laws were very much the same. Of course, there were also important differences, for instance, the reference to a person's nationality as a connecting factor in civil law countries, while the common law, especially in a country of immigration like the United States, used a person's domicile (see 4.3.5.1) instead. The civil law treats a decedent's estate as a whole, while the common law distinguishes between movables and immovables for succession and the law applicable to them (which the current draft of an American Restatement (Third) of Conflict of Laws proposes should be changed to the civil law approach). But the common law, like the civil law, also had definite conflicts rules, often identical ones, and the concept of *stare decisis* (see 4.1.3) provided certainty, predictability, and stability, much the same as codification did in civil law countries.

In the United States (as, of course, in other common law countries), the rules were established by case law. With private law, including conflicts law, being the law of the several individual states, these were appellate and supreme court cases of these states. One might suspect that there were significant differences among the rules of different states. This, however, was not the case, at least not to any great extent.

In the United States, as mentioned earlier, the "Restatements of the Law," prepared by the (private) American Law Institute, review and evaluate the case law of the states in particular fields of law and reduce the result of such review to "rules," along with commentary. The first American "Restatement of the Law – Conflict of Laws" (1932) is the classic (re)statement of the traditional conflicts law; its influence was so great that judicial opinions would rely on and cite to it (rather than to the cases from which it was derived), practically as if it were the same as statutory authority.

The Restatement's rules were definite, strict, without escape, and therefore rigid. Such rigid rules will at times produce patently unjust results. One case may illustrate: A railroad's employee was injured through the negligence of a fellow employee in State B, while all parties were from

State A. The latter would have made the employer railroad liable for its employee's negligence. State B law did not provide for such liability. The State A court, in which the injured employee sued, applied State B law because, as the Restatement also provided, the law of the place of injury is the law applicable to tort liability. Quite obviously, nothing connected the case to State B other than the negligence and resulting injury, while the consequences of the tort were all felt in State A – the injured person's medical expenses, lost earnings, and perhaps State A's need to provide social welfare relief. In those days, none of these contacts of the case with State A was considered a reason to possibly apply the law of State A.

The rationale underlying the traditional system – and bringing about results such as the one reported above – was that rights and obligations "vested" at a time and place when the previously defined fact (here: injury = tort) occurred. The "vested rights" theory ran throughout the system described, and in a way established, by the First Restatement. The reference to the "proper law" in English conflicts usage does not only mean the "applicable law," however that is determined, but also carries with it the notion of an "established" applicable law, in the traditional sense.

4.3.2.1   Escape

The state's highest court could, of course, have changed the precedent in the preceding example. But the place-of-injury rule was too firmly established. Courts wanting to avoid applying a rigid rule that would produce an unjust result designed and resorted to escape devices from *within* the established system. One was to characterize an issue as "procedural," because forum law always governed questions of procedure (see further 4.3.4.1). Thus, when under an old rule a wife could not sue her husband, the local forum might call the issue of "standing to sue" a question of procedure. Characterization could also work in other ways, as in the following illustration: Husband and wife from State A had an accident in State B, and the wife was injured. Back home in A, the wife wants to sue the husband (in order to establish a claim against his insurance), but the state of injury (State B) does not allow a wife to sue her husband in tort. State A's solution? Recharacterize the subject matter: This is not a tort case, but one of family law (interspousal immunity or liability), and family law questions are governed by the law of the spouses' marital domicile – State A. In both of these methods, the court engages in a re-characterization of the issue; it uses characterization as a tool to escape from the basic rule.

Other examples show courts being similarly inventive to achieve particular results without, however, drawing the basic system and its rules into question. In contract, for instance, the contract is made (and the rights and obligations of the parties "vest") upon acceptance of the offer. But it may be open to debate (and to some manipulation) where and when the offer was made and where it was accepted. This was important in early American cases when women were under disability to contract in one state, but not in another, and communications went back and forth between these states.

Escape devices could help to avoid unfavorable results under the rigid rules in some cases. Escape devices were not rules of their own; they were court-improvised reasoning, invented to gain some flexibility. The system itself was not open to flexibility and drew increasing criticism for that rigidity. Changes occurred here and there in the case law of some American states, for instance in New York, but the major turn came with what is now called the American "Conflicts Revolution." It changed American conflicts law fundamentally, and beyond that, has been influential in conflicts law development elsewhere as well.[13]

4.3.3   The American "Conflicts Revolution" and case-specific approaches

In the 1950s and 1960s, a number of theories emerged in the United States, and courts experimented with some of them. Three of them are identified below, of which two are the most influential, and therefore most widely followed today. They will be treated below, while others will be mentioned in passing.

4.3.3.1   *"Governmental interest analysis"*

All conflicts systems, of course, recognize and give effect to their own public interests (and perhaps even those of another state: see below). They do this by applying their own mandatory norm, either to displace the otherwise applicable law or to reject that law, in an individual case,

---

[13]   Peter Hay, "European Conflicts Law After the American 'Revolution' – Comparative Notes", 2015 Eu L. F. 1–10, and 2015 U. Ill. L. Rev. 2053. See also Peter Hay, "On the Road to a Third American Restatement of Conflicts Law," 42 IPRax 205 (2022).

on public policy grounds, as discussed above. But in these cases, the court departs from what is "the otherwise applicable law." There are statutory or case law conflicts rules for the determination of an applicable law, and public interest concerns make for exceptions. The public ("governmental") interest of the forum is not the *means* for the determination of the applicable law in the first place. That is how this approach differs from the "interest analysis" approach.

"Governmental interest analysis" was introduced by the American scholar *Brainerd Currie*. As a methodology in its own right, it is the basis of many American conflicts decisions. Beyond that, it has significantly influenced other American methodologies. To a much more limited extent, it has also influenced modern European developments.

Currie's "governmental interest analysis" is forum-centric, an orientation that has influenced other American approaches, although it is not their core orientation. In contrast, civil law conflicts law is not forum-centric; the American influence on it takes other forms.

An important contribution is *Currie*'s question, at the beginning of his analysis, as to whether the issue presents a "true" or a "false" conflict between the different states' laws. A false conflict exists if the foreign law, although not the same as forum law, is not designed to cover a case such as the one before the court. For instance, in the case of the railroad employee injured through the negligence of a fellow employee (see 4.3.2), the State A court might have asked why there is no liability under State B law. It might have concluded (in its opinion, regardless of whether actually true historically) that State B law is designed to protect State B employers and their insurers against collusive claims by employees, perhaps also to make State B attractive for business. None of these aspects is present in this case: The defendant is a State A employer, and there appears no reason why State B should protect it; nor is B's judicial system to be protected against collusive claims, since the case is in A; and protecting State A employers will not attract businesses to State B. The State A court might therefore have concluded that the case presents a "false conflict." The logical consequence of this conclusion would then have to be that State B law drops out, i.e., it becomes irrelevant, and only State A law remains. Other American approaches would reach the same result, as would EU law. For both, see 4.3.1.1.2.

What if the other law is indeed designed to apply to a case such as the one before the court – if there is a "true conflict" between it and the law of the forum? *Currie* instructs application of forum law, because a court may neither weigh the conflicting states' rules against each other, nor substitute its judgment for that of the forum's lawgiver (whether legislature or precedent-setting higher court).

An American example: an Oregon citizen contracts for a loan in California. The lender is Californian, and the loan is made and to be repaid in California. When the borrower defaults, the lender sues in Oregon. The defendant raises the defense that the borrower had earlier been declared a "spendthrift" (someone unable to handle his or her assets responsibly) and put under guardianship. The guardian invokes the borrower's incapacity and declares the obligation annulled. Both states follow the rule that contracts are to be honored (*pacta sunt servanda*), and everything connects this contract with California. Its law would ordinarily apply, and a California court would hold for the lender. In *Currie* fashion, the Oregon court, faced with a true conflict, formulates that "courts are instruments of state policy,"[14] and finds for the defendant by applying Oregon's law protecting spendthrifts. The court might have dismissed the case, in furtherance of Oregon's protective public policy, which would not permit application of another law, thus leaving the lender free to pursue a remedy elsewhere, where the borrower might have assets. But this court did not. In its view, it may not weigh one law against another; it must follow forum law. It thereby freed the borrower, and deprived the lender of his claim.

Currie does weigh one law against another when the true conflict exists between two other laws, not involving the forum. This need not be pursued further: Suffice it to say that when the forum is involved, the *Currie* formulation of "governmental interest analysis" is forum-centric. One variation, which differs because weighing is involved, is known as the "comparative impairment test." California follows this model. The court is to apply the law of the state whose interests "would be more impaired by not having its law applied." This approach weighs governmental interests against each other. Like *Currie*'s approach, it tends to be forum-centric because the forum is often likely to find itself to be the "more impaired" state.

---

[14]   *Lilienthal v. Kaufman*, 395 P.2d 543, 549 (Or. 1964) (en banc).

4.3.3.2   Better law

Another approach, likewise often forum-centric in result, although expressly not as a matter of lip service, is the "better law approach." Commenting on the built-in temptation to find the better law at home, an eminent British commentator asked, "is there any case in which a court has said 'Our law on this point is a drag on the coat-tails of civilization' …?"[15] Today, only two or three states adopt this approach. However, the Second Restatement facilitates following it, without saying so (see 4.3.3.3).

4.3.3.3   The "most significant relationship": the Second Restatement

American courts experimented with a number of different approaches as they sought to soften the effects of the First Restatement's rigidity. To pull all these developments together, the American Law Institute produced a Second Restatement of conflicts law in 1971. It retained a great number of the traditional rules, followed both in the United States and around the world, such that the *lex sitae* applies to real property. However, it broke new ground with respect to the law applicable in tort and contract. With respect to both, in parallel provisions (§§ 145 and 188, respectively), it calls for the application of the law of the "most significant relationship to the particular issue."

The Second Restatement provides courts with two aids. First, in the respective articles themselves, the Restatement lists a number of connecting factors that should be considered. All are familiar from traditional law, such as place of conduct, place of injury, place of contract negotiation, place of contract performance, and several more. In contrast to traditional law, there is no priority among them; none is a "rule." Instead, the list contains non-prioritized, and indeed open-ended (non-exclusive) "factors."

A second aid is the Second Restatement's section on "General Principles" (§ 6). The contract and tort provisions direct that this section should be used to evaluate the above-mentioned connecting "factors." The "General Principles" include – again, in non-inclusive and non-prioritized form

---

[15]   J.H.C. Morris, "Law and Reason Triumphant or How Not to Review a Restatement", 21 Am. J. Comp. L. 322, 324 (1973) (reviewing Restatement (Second) of Conflict of Laws (1971)).

– the interests of the forum and of the other state, the "smooth working of the interstate system," justified party expectations and interest, ease in the determination and application of a law, the development in an area of law, and so forth. It is clear, even from this brief recitation, that the "General Principles" provide a home for everyone – and everyone's approach. First Restatement adherents may find vested rights covered (certainty, party expectations); the "better law" is covered (development of the area of the law; smooth working of the "interstate and international systems") and "governmental interests" are there (forum interests); and the open-endedness of it all permits giving in to one's own preferences.

4.3.3.4   What is American conflicts law today, especially in tort and contract?

Some ten or so states continue to follow the First Restatement; about three are "better law" states; California follows the "comparative impairment approach"; New York follows rules established in its *Neumeier* decision;[16] and most of the rest of the jurisdictions that make up the United States (individual states, District of Columbia, Puerto Rico, Virgin Islands, and Guam) refer in their tort and contract conflicts decisions to the Second Restatement. As the above discussion illustrates, such a reference is quite meaningless unless one knows what orientation the particular state has adopted in its application of the "General Principles" (see 4.3.3.3). Research with respect to American conflicts law, especially in these two important areas of tort and contract, must therefore go beyond reading the Second Restatement. It requires examination of the case law of the particular state.

Some of the above may make things look chaotic. That, however, would vastly overstate the situation, because it would once again overlook the stability provided by precedent – the rule of *stare decisis*. It is true that conflicts law is still in flux (for instance, as the remaining First Restatement states might consider new approaches). Overall, however, it is quite stable. The difficulty for the foreign observer is that there is no "American" uniformity. As in different countries, there are different methods for determining the applicable law in the different American states. At the same time, it is true that most American approaches are, or

---

[16]   *Neumeier v. Kuehner*, 286 N.E. 2d 454 (N.Y. 1972); *Schultz v. Boy Scouts of America, Inc.*, 480 N.E. 2d 679 (N.Y. 1985) (modifying *Neumeier*).

at least lend themselves to be, forum-centric. This stands in great contrast to EU conflicts law, that of other civil law countries, and even that of common law countries like Australia, Canada, and the United Kingdom. But even forum-centricity has limits: The United States Supreme Court has held that the Federal Constitution's Due Process Clause requires that a case have a significant contact, or a "significant aggregation of contacts," with the forum before a court may apply its own law.[17] Under this test, the Oregon decision in the spendthrift case (discussed at 4.3.3.1) would arguably be unconstitutional today. Other systems (e.g., the EU) and other conflicts laws do not have such an explicit limit, nor do they need one, for none provides a court with the leeway afforded by most American conflicts law.

The last remarks also show why there is no place for a "false conflict/ true conflict" analysis in these other systems, at least not as a matter of methodology. These systems continue to be rule-oriented. The applicable law is predetermined by the rule. Hence, there is no need to search for it. Policy considerations may and do enter in, but not for the determination of the applicable law (except when a mandatory norm provides it). They furnish reasons to depart from it in exceptional circumstances; they are escape clauses. Examples are the displacement of the ordinarily applicable law by a "manifestly more closely" connected other law, or as a result of the public policy exception.

4.3.3.5   The future: the Draft Restatement (Third)

Since 2014, work has been under way in the American Law Institute – the private organization of judges, academics, and lawyers that promulgates Restatements – to draft a Restatement (Third) of Conflict of Laws. A number of proposed sections have already been approved by the Institute's membership, but completion of the project may take additional years.

Like the Restatement (Second), the new Restatement will state some definite rules that courts may adopt. Examples are the new definition of domicile (see 4.3.5.1, adopting the unitary European approach to succession (see 4.6.2.2), using the *Günstigkeitsprinzip* in cases of environmental damage (see 4.3.1.1.2), and formulating some tort rules on the basis of

---

[17]   *Allstate Ins. Co. v. Hague*, 449 U.S. 302, 313 (1981).

distinguishing conduct-regulating rules from those that are loss allocating. When no specific rule has been suggested, courts should determine the "scope" of the possibly applicable laws and, if more than one is applicable and rules conflict, apply the "most appropriate law" or the law of the state with the "dominant interest." The "scope" determination more or less corresponds with *Currie*'s and the current law's "false conflict" analysis (see 4.3.3.1). The general, residuary, reference to the "most appropriate law" and the list of factors to be considered for that determination remind of the Second Restatement's "most significant relationship" test (see 4.3.3.3 and see 4.3.4.2). The definite rules (including proposed changes) will be welcome improvements if adopted by the courts of the individual states (see 1.3.4). Whether current case law, developed under the Second Restatement's general residuary rule, will really change when there is no express rule and the new residuary rule applies, remains to be seen.[18]

4.3.4 Applicable law for the whole or only part of the case?

4.3.4.1 *Characterization*

When a court seeks to determine what law applies and is directed by its conflicts law to foreign law, will it now import the foreign law wholesale, in a way deciding the case as if it were the foreign court itself? It will not. All legal systems agree that the forum always uses its own procedure and applies the foreign law only to "substantive" matters. They "characterize" a provision of foreign law as either "procedural" or "substantive." For instance, all legal systems have statutes of limitations, setting a date after which a claim is barred. Is the foreign limitation one of "procedure" (its courts are closed after the expiration of the time set by its statute), or is it a matter of "substance" (the claim is extinguished, it no longer exists, cannot be brought anymore anywhere, even in a state with a longer statute)? Countries differ in how they characterize different legal provisions. Civil law countries traditionally characterize statutes of limitations as substantive, while some common law countries, notably, historically, the United States, have characterized them as procedural.

What happens when two countries' characterizations differ? An old German case[19] illustrates the difficulty. According to German conflicts

---

[18]   For further discussion, see Hay, *supra* n. 13 (*On the Road* ...).
[19]   Reichsgericht [RG] [German Supreme Court] Jan. 4, 1882, 7 RGZ 21.

law, Tennessee (United States) law applied to the case. Under the statute of limitations of both states, the claim would be time-barred. Tennessee's conflicts law characterized limitations as procedural, while German law characterized them as substantive. The German court did not apply foreign procedural law, and since Tennessee law governed the substance, it did not apply its substantive limitation. Such an analysis gives the claim eternal life, while a similar domestic claim would have been time-barred in either system. How to solve the dilemma? By not engaging in a double characterization as above, but by characterizing the legal rule in question under the conflicts rule of the forum. In the above example, the German court, calling limitations "substantive," should have applied the Tennessee limitation, regardless of how Tennessee characterizes it. Likewise, had the case arisen in Tennessee, that court should have applied its procedural limitation, regardless of the German view that the limitation, like other aspects of this reverse case, should be governed by Germany's substantive limitation.

Characterization also identifies the subject matter for which an applicable law must be determined. In this context, characterization may help to escape from the unwanted result of an otherwise applicable conflicts rule. An example in 4.3.2.1 illustrates this.

Characterization continues to be important in rule-based conflicts systems, whether in civil law or common law countries. The EU Regulations discussed above, as well as those in other subject areas, contain provisions detailing what issues are subject to the particular Regulation's provisions, in other words, which are "substantive" for EU conflicts law purposes. The lists of these provisions contain time limitations as well as damages, both of which may well be characterized as "procedural" in American law (see further 4.5). Similarly, the American states that still follow the rule-oriented system of the First Restatement need to engage in characterization to determine how much of the foreign law to apply, to which their rule directs them.

In contrast, characterization may play a far less important role under the modern American approaches, in which the law applicable to substantive law issues is itself in flux. The next subsection explains further.

4.3.4.2   Splitting a case into its component issues: dépeçage

The previous subsection showed that potentially applicable foreign law does not apply to every aspect of the case – matters of procedure (how the case moves through the forum's court system) are always governed by forum law. Does the foreign law then apply to *all* substantive aspects of the case? It depends. Here, there is a significant difference between the civil law and many common law systems on the one hand, and American conflicts law on the other.

The Rome I and II Regulations, for instance, refer to "*the* contract" and "*the* non-contractual obligation" (tort), and a provision lists all of the aspects covered by the particular regulation, which are therefore "substantive" as part of "the" contract or tort. There are isolated exceptions, for instance when a mandatory norm of forum law displaces a rule of the otherwise applicable law but leaves other aspects of the latter intact. The Rome I Regulation's provision on party autonomy permits the parties, in stipulating the applicable law, to submit part of their contract to another law. Similarly, the damage provision of EU law, while substantive, directs the court also to consider the victim's home law. Exceptions to the basic orientation to deal with the substantive aspects of the case as a whole thus are specific and few. The focus is on "the" contract, tort, or whatever. This is the basic approach of civil law countries generally, but also for most common law countries that seek to determine the "proper law" applicable to the case.

The matter is different in American conflicts law. Not having an underlying rule orientation (except for those suggested by the non-binding Restatement), its approach is case-specific. To some scholars, the approach to choice of law in a specific individual case should be "consequences-based."[20] While already part of the "governmental interest" approach (comparing policies and purposes expressed in apparently conflicting laws), the Second Restatement makes it express: The applicable law is to be determined for *each* "issue." So does the Draft Restatement (Third). Both their general tort and contract provisions specifically call for the review and application of connecting factors provided in non-exclusive lists, their evaluation in light of the equally open-ended

---

[20]   See Russell J. Weintraub, *Commentary on the Conflict of Laws* § 6.2 et seq. (6th ed., Foundation Press, 2010).

General Principles, with respect to each "issue," and evaluation of the results in light of the "relative weight with respect to each issue." The issue-by-issue approach is known by the French term "*dépeçage*," or "splitting." It is readily apparent that this splitting goes far beyond the substance–procedure characterization (treating the latter under forum law): It takes the *substantive* aspects of the case apart. Open-ended as the approach of the Second Restatement and the Draft Restatement (Third) (and the approaches they accommodate) already is, this issue-by-issue approach affords additional opportunity (subject to the stability provided by *stare decisis*) to reach individualized, not to say *ad hoc*, decisions.

As mentioned at the end of the preceding subsection, the issue-by-issue approach, used in the framework of the Second Restatement's loose "most significant relationship test," also reduces the importance of traditional characterization. It may still prove to be an easy way to get to forum law in the traditional way (for matters styled "procedural"). The potential forum-centricity that the Second and Draft Third Restatements' approaches make possible also may lead to forum law for aspects traditionally considered "substantive" and to be governed by another law. When forum-centricity leads to forum law as the applicable law, there are no aspects of foreign law left to be characterized.

4.3.5   Connecting factors, especially "domicile" and "habitual residence"

In all conflicts systems, there must be something to connect a case or issue to a country to raise the question whether its law should be applied. In the United States, it is indeed unconstitutional for a state to apply its own law unless the case has a significant contact to that state (see 4.3.3.4). Such a constitutional limit is not needed in rule-based conflicts systems, in which application of a rule is triggered by a specified connection. "Connection" can be any fact or conduct, for instance, injury in tort, the stipulated place of performance in contract, or the place of incorporation or principal place of business for a corporation. Rule-based systems contain the required connecting factors as part of the rule. The American Second Restatement's general tort and contract provisions, in contrast, list non-exclusive connecting factors (that is, only illustratively: see 4.3.3.3), potentially making it difficult to foresee what circumstance will be regarded as a relative factor for the determination of the law of the state of the "most significant relationship."

For natural persons, "domicile" (in the common law) and "habitual residence" (in the civil and the common law) have been important connecting factors, with "habitual residence" perhaps gaining ground. Especially in several civil law countries (as countries of emigration), the older reference to a person's nationality, in particular, but not only, for family and succession matters, is still followed as national conflicts law. However, it is generally not followed anymore in conventions or regional law, as in the EU. At most, a nationality connection may give additional weight to another connecting factor, for instance when EU law shortens the required local residence (waiting) period for an ex parte divorce for a person who is also a forum national.

4.3.5.1   Domicile

What law applies to inheritance, with respect to movable property, when the decedent did not leave a will? When does a person from another state get voting rights in a new state of the United States to which he or she has moved? What is the law applicable to a consumer transaction in the EU (see 4.3.1.1.1)? The answers may be "domicile" or "habitual residence" of the decedent at the time of death for the first question, "domicile" or "residence" for the second, and "habitual residence" of the consumer at the time of the transaction for the third. "Domicile" and "habitual residence" are used to define a particularly close relation of the person to the state. In contrast, "residence" is often also tied to a time period, so as to exclude a mere sojourn or other temporary presence. The above examples show the use of these terms in the choice-of-law context. However, it will be remembered that they are also used for judicial jurisdiction over persons: "present" in the state's territory (United States), domiciled or habitually resident in the state, though temporarily absent (United States, EU, and many other civil law systems).

"Domicile" is a uniquely common law concept, with some difference between American and English definitions and practice. Both agree that at any time a person can have only one domicile – an important distinction from "residence," of which a person might have several. In both systems, a person starts with a "domicile of origin," derivative from the (custodial) parent. After attaining capacity, a person may adopt a "domicile of choice" by abandoning the previous domicile, arriving at the new, and having the intent to stay there indefinitely (or, stated differently, with no present intent to leave). This applies for every subsequent change.

In the American view, the present domicile continues until the new one is established. In the English view, when a person leaves a domicile of choice, the "domicile of origin" revives until the new domicile of choice is established.

An example illustrates the difference in approach to change of domicile. An Englishman immigrates to America and settles in Iowa, where he lives and works all of his life. These facts permit the conclusion that Iowa was his domicile. At retirement, he decides to resettle in France. On the trip to France, he dies intestate, leaving personal (movable) property in both Iowa and England. Under both Iowa and English law, the domicile at death applies to intestate succession to movable property. But where was the decedent domiciled? In the American view, he had left Iowa with no intent to return, but he had not yet reached the intended new domicile. His Iowa domicile therefore continued until he reached the new. In the English view, his English domicile revived upon his leaving Iowa; a French domicile had not been perfected. Thus, English and Iowa courts would apply different inheritance laws to his respective local movable property. However, if all interested parties (potential heirs) would participate in either court's proceeding, they would be bound, and the other country's court would recognize that judgment, even though – had the case first been pending in it – it would have applied a different law, and other people might have inherited different amounts – or not all. For the binding effect of a judgment (*res judicata*), see 5.6.1.

Another basic problem with the domicile concept, the above problem apart, is its emphasis on the thought process of the domiciliary. A party must intend to remain indefinitely at a place before one can conclude that it is (or was) his domicile. What if, in the above example, the decedent had indeed reached France before dying? What if, before leaving Iowa, he had also toyed with the idea of ultimately settling in Italy? Where was his domicile at death? It depends on his intent to stay in France *indefinitely*, rather than to be there on his way to Italy. In many such cases, in which the person's actual intent cannot be determined, external facts must be evaluated and interpreted. Obviously, different courts can come to different conclusions.

The Draft Restatement (Third) proposes to retain the domicile concept for judicial jurisdiction and choice-of-law purposes but to define it in terms of "where a person's life is centered," considering familial, social, economic, religious, and other aspects of a person's life. The definition thus focusses on objective facts and eliminates a reference to a person's subjective intent (which can also often be surmised only by considering objective facts).

4.3.5.2 Habitual residence

Because of the possible difficulty of determining intent to establish "domicile," it seems preferable to use another test to establish whether a person's connection to a country is close enough to warrant application of its law to such a question as intestate succession, as in the previous example. In much modern conflicts legislation, as in the Rome I and II Regulations, "habitual residence" is now the test. Interestingly enough, the Brussels Ia Regulation on jurisdiction (see 3.2) still uses "domicile" in its English-language version. However, that term has been given the meaning of "habitual residence" (rather than picking up the English legal concept). Indeed, England has provided by legislation that, for use in its courts, "domicile" for purposes of Brussels Ia means residence of at least six months.

While "habitual residence," on the face of it, is no more definite or easy to apply, the lack of the subjective, often impossible-to-determine, intent element is a major improvement. The English legislation is one instance of making the concept more concrete. The same test – six months – can now be found in other contexts; for instance, the interstate uniform laws on child custody and support, as well as the Hague Child Abduction Convention (see 3.6.4), use it in determining a child's "home state."

It is thus quite clear that "habitual residence," unlike mere "residence," but very much like the basic notion underlying "domicile," means a person's presence of some permanence, with the latter's length, as mentioned, repeatedly stated as something like six months. Even when a law uses only the term "residence," it will be given a meaning requiring some permanence. For instance, the United States Constitution provides in its Fourteenth Amendment that in addition to being a United States citizen, a person is also a citizen "of the State wherein [he] reside[s]." Since there cannot be multiple state citizenships derived from multiple residences, that term also requires domicile-like permanence in view of its context.

4.3.5.3   *Domicile of juridical persons*

In the current (traditional) law, a juridical person's (e.g., a business organization's) equivalent to a natural person's domicile for choice-of-law purposes is its state of incorporation or principal place of business. The Draft Restatement (Third) complicates matters a little by expressly introducing *dépeçage* (above at 4.3.4.2) into the determination: a juridical person's domicile is its principal place of business with respect to the "particular choice of law issue." Depending on the issue (for instance, contract formation), the juridical person's domicile equivalent may thus differ from case to case.[21]

4.4   Renvoi

Every country's law, of course, also contains its conflicts law (its choice-of-law rules). Does a reference to a country's substantive law as being the law applicable to a case or issue also include that country's conflicts law? If it does, the forum court would then be following that law's reference and decide the case in the same way as the court to which its law refers.

There are three possibilities as to what can happen if the other state's conflicts law is considered as part of the reference to its substantive law: (1) the foreign choice-of-law rule refers to its own country: forum and foreign law agree that the foreign law should apply; (2) the foreign choice-of-law rule refers to forum law – in other words it refers back, a situation called *remission*, about which there is more below; (3) the foreign choice-of-law rule refers to yet another, a third state, a situation called *transmission*. The whole subject matter of considering the foreign choice-of-law rules for possible remissions or transmissions is known by its French name: *renvoi*.

Can *renvoi* contribute to a uniform result? Take the case of a person who is a citizen of State A, dying intestate domiciled in State B, and leaving movable assets (for instance, bank accounts) in the United States (State

---

[21]   A comment on § 2.08 of the Draft states that the new provision is not to replace the law of the state of incorporation for "intra-corporate disputes" (the so-called "internal affairs rule"). The U.S. Supreme Court had applied the latter in *CTS Corp. v. Dynamics Corp. of Am.*, 481 U.S. 69 (1987).

C). Under uniform American conflicts law, inheritance of the American assets is governed by the law of the state of domicile at death (here, State B). Assume that State B is a civil law state, and still follows the civil law rule of applying the law of nationality (State A), and that State A has the same rule as State B. The American court (State C), deciding who gets the decedent's assets, could achieve a uniform result by employing *renvoi*: It would refer to State B under its own conflicts law, follow the transmission to State A, and come up with the same result as States A and B would. If the State C court did not engage in *renvoi*, it would be applying State B law, which neither State B nor State A would do.

Take an example of remission: The decedent is an American citizen (State A), dying domiciled in State B, leaving movable property in State A. The forum (State A) looks to State B, which looks to the law of the country of the decedent's nationality (State A), in other words, back to State A. If both countries use *renvoi*, this could then go back and forth – a ping-pong game, a merry-go-round. A uniform result cannot be achieved; it would be possible only if one country engaged in *renvoi* and the other did not.

Does using the other state's conflicts law make sense in these circumstances? Since a uniform result cannot be reached, the forum could cut off the reference when it comes back to the forum and apply its own law. It is always easier to apply one's own law because no interests of the other country are affected; it also considered the law of the forum to be applicable. This last aspect also shows that the issue really presents a "false conflict" (see 4.3.3.1): The foreign law becomes irrelevant, and forum law applies.

Many civil law systems employed *renvoi* traditionally, but the United States did not, even though the Second Restatement recommended its use when doing so would aid in achieving a uniform result (see the transmission example above). Recently, countries that previously used *renvoi* are abandoning it. Thus, for instance, the EU Rome I and II Regulations expressly guide against the use of another country's choice-of-law rules. This means that the forum's reference to another law is a reference to that other country's (substantive) law, minus that country's procedural and conflicts law.

On the other hand, the EU's Succession Regulation provides for *renvoi* if the reference to the other state's conflicts law is to the law of another EU

Member State, or to a third state that would apply its own law. Other civil law systems also continue to use *renvoi* in the context of succession.

American courts have generally rejected *renvoi*, and the Restatement (Second) recommended its use only in exceptional cases. The Draft Restatement (Third) rejects it expressly except when the forum and the other involved state's policy seek to achieve a uniform result. That excludes remission and leaves only the relatively rare cases of transmission by both involved states to a third.

But the result which remission might bring about may also be reached in another way. Consideration of the other involved state's conflicts law may display a reference to the forum rather than to itself or to another state. It thus considers its own law inapplicable: The case thus presents a "false conflict," and forum law can be applied without further analysis. There is no need then to determine, for example, which is the country with the "most significant relationship" to the case or issue. The result accords with the policies of both states: The forum follows its conflicts rule and does what the state would do if it had the case. Remission and false-conflicts analysis come to this result. So far, however, the Draft Restatement (Third) rejects consideration of another state's conflicts law for a determination of the "scope" (see above at 4.3.3.5) of that state's substantive law. This may bring about a result that the law of neither state intended.

4.5   Special aspects in American law regarding time limits, damages

Time limitations and damages were discussed earlier in the context of characterization. Both are usually characterized as "substantive" in civil law systems, but often as "procedural" in common law systems, especially in American states. Some further details deserve mention.

4.5.1   Time limitations

The general rule in American conflicts law is indeed that time limitations are "procedural," although a revision of the relevant Second Restatement rule does contemplate the opposite characterization in limited circumstances. It will be remembered that the "most significant relationship" approach of the Second Restatement already permits an individualized approach, although a "homeward trend" amounts to the same as a "procedural" characterization. In application of the so-called "borrowing statutes," the forum "borrows" (applies) the other state's shorter statute, the same as if it were "substantive." This prevents prosecution of stale claims under the applicable substantive law.

Another departure from the general rule occurs when the foreign time limitation appears to be "built in," that is, it appears to be intimately part of the particular cause of action, as distinguished from a general, all claims-encompassing limitation. This will often be the case when the particular claim was unknown to the common law, but was created by statute, and the latter also contains the time limitation. Wrongful death and product liability statutes are examples.

4.5.2   Damages

The previous paragraph also applies to damages: They may also be "built in" the statute that creates the claim, for instance, when a statute provides for a cause of action for wrongful death (unknown to the common law) with damages limited to a certain amount. For both time limitation (above) and statutory damage limitation cases, it may be said that the claim created by the statute exists only within the parameters (limitations) of the statute. There may be a difference, however, in the case of damages when the new cause of action exists in both the foreign and the forum state. As to liability, there is no conflict; application of forum law would impose no new liability (in the way that application of the forum's longer statute of limitations would). However, it would impose a different – namely, larger – liability by applying its own law with a higher ceiling, or perhaps none at all.

There is American case law, however, that would not consider the foreign damage limit to be "built in" and therefore would not follow such a limit. These cases reject the foreign limitation on public policy grounds when the forum provides for unlimited liability. As in other cases where local public policy speaks against the result that application of the foreign law would produce, it seems preferable to dismiss the case, rather than entertain it and thereby export one's own law.

It deserves brief mention that not all damages serve compensatory purposes (whether for actual injury and associated expenses or for consequential emotional injury or loss of earnings). Damages may also be awarded to deter similar conduct, or to reward a plaintiff for prosecuting a case in the public interest, for instance, an antitrust violation. The latter are "punitive damages," also "exemplary damages" in English law. (See 3.4, with respect to class actions.) Punitive damages are unknown to the civil law: Punishment belongs to the criminal law and has no place in civil litigation. Later discussion will return to this difference, in the context of the recognition of a foreign judgment that awards punitive damages (see 5.5.5.1).

4.6   Choice of law in areas other than contract or tort

4.6.1   Family law

Many, if not most, family law issues arise as preliminary or incidental questions in other contexts. Examples include whether a foreign marriage should be recognized for purposes of settling a decedent's estate or for succession to pension rights as a "surviving spouse;" determining what matrimonial property regime applies, again, for purposes of inheritance or for post-divorce allocation of assets; and determining whether one spouse is responsible for the debts of the other. Rarely, therefore, will a status question arise by itself, such as "Are A and B married?"

4.6.1.1   Capacity

Capacity to marry is traditionally governed by the couple's "personal law" which, in the civil law, was (and often still is) each prospective spouse's nationality. Illustration: X, a citizen of State A, which does not recognize divorce, obtains a divorce from the current spouse in State B and now wishes to marry Y, who has always been single, in State C, which follows the nationality principle. Upon application for a marriage license, State C determines that Y has capacity, but X does not because, under the law of his or her citizenship (that of State A), X is not single. Assuming, however, that State C had recognized the divorce (see also 3.6.3), had issued a marriage license (regarding both X and Y as single), and they had then been married there, it is likely that even State A would recognize the marriage in application of the law of celebration (*lex celebrationis*).

Common law systems usually apply forum law with respect to capacity (e.g., degrees of consanguinity, ability to enter a same-sex marriage, minimum age, single status as viewed by forum law), as State C did in the last example. These requirements may, of course, vary from country to country, and that may invite forum shopping. Underage persons may get married in a neighboring state with a lower age requirement, or a same-sex couple may marry in a jurisdiction providing for this, although they are residents or nationals of a state either not providing same-sex marriage or indeed prohibiting it. Both types of forum shopping occurred in the United States. The Uniform Marriage Evasion Act[22] provided for non-recognition by the home state when the underage couple returned there. It was one of the less successful uniform acts, having been adopted by only five states. Another provision of the Act was used by Massachusetts when it was the first American state providing for same-sex marriage: It would grant marriage licenses only to those whose home state also provided for such a marriage and would therefore recognize the Massachusetts marriage rather than refuse to recognize it, as permitted by American federal law at the time. Today, same-sex marriage is available throughout the United States. For the 2022 Protection for Marriage Act see Section 3.6.2. The earlier forum-shopping problem is now moot there, but it is not throughout the world, as many countries do not recognize same-sex marriages and some even prohibit them as a matter of criminal law.

4.6.1.2   Forms of marriage

The previous sections discussed capacity to marry – and the related issue of recognition of a marriage – in the context of traditional civil marriages, though they, of course, differ in detail around the world. To this may be added the private (non-official) marriage, and religious marriages, such as Jewish, Islamic, and Hindu marriages, or those according to some tribal rights. These may or may not require some subsequent official registration. An example of a private marriage is the American common law marriage (see 3.6.2), in which a couple lives as husband and wife and

---

[22]   9A U.L.A. 21 (1957) (withdrawn by the National Conference of Commissioners on Uniform State Laws in 1970).

is regarded as "married" by the community. Common law marriages have been abolished in many but not all American states, but they are recognized even in a state where one cannot be formed locally, if valid where entered and lived. However different all these forms are, the basic reference to and application of the *lex celebrationis* assures their recognition, and thereby protects the parties in their expectations.

4.6.1.3   Marital property

Who owns what in (and after) a marriage? Parties will enter a marriage, a civil union, or other formalized relationship with property that each had acquired earlier. Does the new spouse or partner acquire any claim to that property as a result of the marriage? What about further income produced by that property, such as stock dividends or rental income? During the marriage, when one or both of the spouses or partners work, do they share in each other's income? Conversely, do they share debts, so that one may be responsible for the debts of the other?

When all is well, these questions rarely arise; they are abstract. They become important when a spouse dies, or if they should divorce, or if one becomes insolvent. In the case of death, a will may provide for the survivor – but there may not be a will, or a will may provide very little. Then, questions arise: Might the spouse not already own part of the assets by virtue of the marriage? Might statutory provisions also apply and give relief? Much the same questions arise upon divorce: How much of the assets does each spouse already own? Should one spouse share his or her own property with the other, or possibly pay continuing maintenance?

Legal systems use different ways to protect spouses when their union ends. They may provide that property is shared equally (all property, or only property acquired during marriage?) so that there is no need to make additional provision for a party upon divorce or the death of the other. In contrast, other systems individualize and look at each spouse's property separately. When spouses differ in earnings (or one has neither income from employment nor another source of income), there will often be a need to provide for the survivor or divorcee by law.

In the United States, both systems of marital property prevail – the traditional common law model (separate property of the spouses) and the community property system. The latter has been adopted by nine states, is optional in a tenth, and is modelled after civil law concepts. The former applies in the remaining states. Under both systems (also true in many civil law countries), property acquired by a spouse before the marriage is his or her "separate property." The same is true of property subsequently acquired by gift or inheritance. In the "common law" system, this separation also extends to most property acquired by each spouse individually *during* marriage. Obviously, there is then a need for a provision, after marriage, for a spouse who never acquired equivalent (or any) means of his or her own.

In a "community property" state, pre-marital separate property remains separate, but property acquired during marriage belongs to both, half-and-half. Property acquired during marriage is said to belong to the "community," in which each spouse has an undivided one-half interest. The nature of movable property – whether it is separate or part of the community – is determined by the domicile of the acquiring spouse at the time of acquisition. In the case of real property, the law of the situs determines its nature.

Under both systems, it is possible to change the form of the property without changing its nature. For example, one spouse might use the proceeds from selling an automobile, which she or he inherited, to purchase a motorcycle. The motorcycle would also be that spouse's separate property, so long as it was acquired with the proceeds from the sale (or other separate property; the automobile was so because it was acquired by inheritance). A subsequent acquisition is said to be "traced" into the property used for its acquisition; the nature of the spousal property interest does not change.

Consider property that produces income for its owner: Should that income be assigned the nature – separate or community – of the underlying property? Stated differently, should the income produced by an asset take the same nature as that of the underlying asset? The laws of the 50 US states do not agree on this point. The general rule used to be that the income maintains the nature of the property from which it was derived, but exceptions – not to mention *ad hoc* adjustments by courts undertaking to distribute assets equitably on a case-by-case basis – nearly swallow the rule whole.

In the previous two examples, it is important to keep in mind that the form of the transaction can affect the ultimate result. For example, had the proceeds from the sale of the automobile, above, been added to a joint checking account, held by both spouses, before being used to purchase the motorcycle, those separate funds would arguably become community property, as would the motorcycle purchased with them. Had the proceeds from the sale been kept separate, perhaps in a non-joint account, then there would be no such question as to their nature.

Conflicts problems arise when spouses change their domicile to another country, or even to another American state. An example is the problem of inheritance rights when the two systems protect spouses in different ways. The common law gives the surviving spouse at least a "statutory" share of the decedent's (separate) property (unless a will provides for more), while a community property state does not grant an inheritance right because the survivor already owns half. It could therefore happen that a decedent, domiciled in a community property state at death but having only previously acquired separate property, leaves the survivor with nothing. This is so because the decedent's domicile at death determines succession to movables, and a community property state gives no claim against separate property. California and some other states have found a way out of this unfortunate result by statute: They regard as community property everything that *would have been* community property, had it been acquired within their state (so-called "quasi-community property"). This concept still does not protect a spouse *during* marriage, for instance, if the partner should give away or squander his or her separate property.

Obviously, spouses can arrange their property relations through joint accounts or the like during their lifetime or by will. But the "statutory share" in common law marital property states and the "quasi-community property" concept in community property states assure that the surviving spouse cannot be left with nothing, including as a result of an attempt to reduce his or her share by will.

Civil law countries reach similar results, though the conceptualization of how spouses are protected may be different. The German system, adapted from the French, which provides for the splitting of each party's "accrued gains" during marriage, in essence produces the same result as the American "community property" system. A comparison of the value of a party's assets before and at the end of the marriage will disclose the gain that has "accrued" to each. Compared with and in relation to the other party's gain, one will end up showing a surplus and the other a deficit, calling for equalization. Here too, some gains are not counted in the calculation, such as gifts and inheritances (simply because the marital relationship had nothing to do with their coming about). German law provides parties with other choices, for instance, it allows an agreement to have all of their property (whether acquired before or during the marriage) treated as common (community) property, entitling each to one-half. Needless to say, the same is, of course, possible in common law countries: The statutory rules are default rules, within which parties can arrange their property relations as they wish (limited only by the protective nature of the common law "statutory share").

The foregoing has assumed that the court's national law applied. That need not be true, of course. While the common law looks to the domicile of the party at the time of acquisition, other countries show a number of different approaches to choice of law. The German Civil Code, as well as other laws such as the Polish, still look to the law of the parties' common nationality (followed by other references if their nationalities differ). Others, such as the French, may look to the parties' first common habitual residence as a couple, in keeping with the approach of a Hague Convention. Still others – closer to the common law – may look to the parties' habitual residence at the time of acquisition (thereby also avoiding having to deal with the common law's concept of "domicile," which may be difficult to apply: see 4.3.5.1). All systems, though with different limitations, allow parties to choose the law applicable to their property relationship.

All of the above approaches were, of course, designed to apply to the property relationship of parties to a traditional marriage. In countries that provide for same-sex marriage, these rules also apply to parties to such a marriage. But what of other same-sex relationships, such as registered partnerships? Here the answer is unclear. Some systems liken such unions to traditional marriages, for instance for purposes of inheritance. Others may lack developed rules. The EU has led the way by establishing a definite rule for registered partnerships: Unless the parties make specific other arrangements (joint title to property, for instance), the law applicable to their property regime is that of the state of registration of their union.

Conflict problems can also arise when cultural differences require a state to deal with a legal concept of another state that is unknown to its own legal system. A good example is the *mahr* of Islamic marriage practice: The husband-to-be promises a gift of money or other valuables to the wife-to-be as part of their agreement to marry. Is the *mahr* to be evaluated as part of their matrimonial property arrangement, and if so, how (community or her separate property)? Or is it a promise in lieu of a support obligation or of inheritance rights? Courts have not given uniform answers to this problem.

4.6.1.4   Support

An earlier section (see 3.6.5) addressed jurisdictional issues with respect to support – both child support and post-marital maintenance for a divorced spouse. What law applies? Very often, the suit will be brought where the claimant lives. When the defendant is not subject to that court's jurisdiction, judicial cooperation – both interstate in the United States and internationally through a Hague Convention or bilateral mechanisms (see 3.6.5) – will reach the maintenance debtor at his or her residence, through a court exercising jurisdiction there. In civil law jurisdictions, such as the EU, the claimant's court may proceed to exercise jurisdiction over an absent debtor even without the help of a court at the latter's residence. As noted, a judgment based on such far-reaching exercise of jurisdiction would face recognition difficulties in the United States (see 3.6.5).

There is, however, common agreement that the applicable law is generally that of the claimant's domicile or habitual residence. That, after all, is the place where the need for support is felt. This is also the rule adopted by the 2007 Hague Protocol on the Law Applicable to Maintenance Obligations,[23] ratified by the EU on behalf of its member countries (except Denmark and the United Kingdom), Brazil, Ecuador, Kazakhstan, Serbia, and Ukraine (as of 2022). The Protocol also provides that the applicable law changes as the claimant's domicile changes. Again, this makes sense from the perspective of the claimant's needs; however, only so long as sufficient attention and weight is given to the debtor's needs and financial capability.

---

[23]   November 23, 2007, available at: https://www.hcch.net/en/instruments/conventions/full-text/?cid=133 (accessed March 6, 2018).

In connection with spousal post-divorce support in the United States, it is interesting to note that in common law states the older concept of alimony (i.e., periodic support payments) has often been replaced by "equitable division" of property. While not exactly the same as property division in a community property state, this approach comes close to it.

4.6.2   Succession

4.6.2.1   Introduction

Inheritance laws provide more than just a mechanism for the orderly transfer of wealth from one generation to the next. In the manner in which they regulate such intergenerational transfers, they also pursue important social objectives: Who should be protected against being disinherited (ignored) by the testator (only immediate family members like the spouse and children, or also beyond, to include distant relatives)? Should standards of protection be the same in testate and in intestate succession (or give the testator greater freedom in testate succession)? What is or should be the effect of a couple's marital property regime on a spouse's right to inherit from the other (see the discussion of community property in the United States and the Islamic *mahr*, at 4.6.1.3)? Decedents may leave property, both real and personal, in any number of states or countries; do different laws apply in each jurisdiction, or will all assets (the "estate" of the decedent) be governed by a single law, even though the laws of the different states may reflect different policies? And how does it all work procedurally?

4.6.2.2   Procedural issues

Common law and civil law differ in one very important respect: How does the decedent's property pass – directly to the testamentary or statutory heirs, or first to an intermediary? One consequence of how this question is answered concerns the decedent's debts: Do the heirs inherit them along with the assets, or do they get paid by the intermediary, so that the heirs receive what is left, debt-free? In the civil law, the heirs take directly, but can decline the inheritance in the face of debts. In the common law, the decedent's property passes to his or her "estate" ("The Estate of [Name]"), which is administered by the *executor*, whom the decedent named in his or her will or, in the case of intestacy, by an *administrator* appointed by the probate court. The latter collects the assets, pays the debts, accounts to the court, and with the court's approval, makes distributions to the heirs.

A second major difference is that the civil law treats the decedent's assets as a whole, while the common law distinguishes between real and personal (movable) property, a distinction that also has effect on the applicable law (situs law applies to immovable, the law of domicile at death to movable property). Not treating the estate as a whole will also mean that inheritance procedures may be needed wherever there are assets (even if ultimately the same law is applicable in each). Thus, in the United States, there is a principal (or domiciliary) administration at the decedent's domicile at death and ancillary administration wherever other personal property is located. The situs deals with real property situated there. In such a system, creditors may need to file their claims in all places where there is administration, lest local assets in one place prove insufficient. Inter-court cooperation may alleviate this by establishing the overall value of the assets and of the claims, arriving at an overall percentage of satisfaction, and having local administrations achieve this by transfers among them (in essence, carrying over principles of bankruptcy law).

In the United States, the Draft Restatement (Third) (see 4.6.2.2) proposes the adoption of the European unitary approach to succession rather than to adhere to the scission of the traditional common law. Especially in a country with more than fifty different domestic jurisdictions, this would be a welcome change. However, given the fact that conflicts law is the individual law of each domestic jurisdiction, each state's highest court would still need to agree and then adopt the proposed new approach as part of that state's law.

In a (civil law) system that regards the decedent's estate as a whole and provides for the heir's direct succession (without an intermediary in the form of another legal person, i.e., the "Estate of …"), there is still a need and a role for a court, often a chamber of the court of first instance. It oversees the opening of the decedent's will, if any, receives an heir's rejection of the inheritance (see above), and may order sequestration and administration of the decedent's assets, for instance, on application of a creditor who fears that the heirs will not responsibly satisfy them, or that assets may become dissipated. Overall, however, common law probate courts are often more extensively involved in the winding-up of a decedent's estate.

4.6.2.3   Applicable law

What law applies to a testator's capacity to make a will, to the formal requirements for a valid will, to the determination of who inherits and how much, and in the absence of a will, to the possible application of yet a different law for the protection of certain persons? With respect to these issues, the two large legal systems – civil law and common law – are quite alike in their approach. (The following leaves aside rules that are specific to religious laws, and in such cases, may displace or exist side by side with state (civil) law.) Of the foregoing, only one issue – the "Form of Testamentary Disposition" – has been addressed by an international convention, the Hague Convention of 1961,[24] adopted by over fifty countries (as of 2022), including EU countries, but not the United States. Like many national conflicts laws, the Convention provides for four different possible laws for movable property, in addition to situs law for immovable property, so that, if the conditions of one of them are met, the will is regarded as validly made. These options are designed to effectuate the intent of the testator in every way possible, to thereby prevent the will from failing on formal grounds. (For party autonomy in the EU, see 4.3.1.1.1.)

All other issues remain a matter of national conflicts laws (except for the EU, see 4.1.2). These laws are essentially similar, despite procedural differences in the way that succession is administered. All seek to identify a single law, except for common law countries, which distinguish between movable and immovable property, with potentially different laws applying to each category. In the United States, the Draft Restatement (Third) proposes a change to the civil law system (see 4.6.2.3). Civil law countries do not distinguish between movable and immovable property. They will usually apply a single law to the entire estate but may have difficulty in accepting another state's succession decision involving real property in their own country (for more, see 4.6.2.5). At least for movable property, most countries apply a single law: Traditionally, in the civil law (but now changed under EU law for its members), it was the law of the decedent's nationality; in common law countries, predictably, the reference was to the law of the decedent's domicile at death. More recently, the latter reference has become almost universally adopted.

---

[24]   Convention on the Conflicts of Laws Relating to the Form of Testamentary Dispositions, Oct. 5, 1961, 510 U.N.T.S. 175.

All systems provide protection for some parties, for instance, the "forced share" of the surviving spouse in a common law state (but not a community property state: see 4.6.1.3) and similar rights in civil law countries, such as the "statutory right" under German law or the *legitime* under French law. The persons protected and the nature and extent of their claims and rights will, of course, differ from country to country, and this may become important in the context of recognition in international succession cases (discussed at 4.6.2.5).

4.6.2.4 EU law

In the EU, its Succession Regulation of 2012 (see also 5.5.6) contains novel and forward-looking provisions. It adopts the civil law approach of dealing with the decedent's estate "as a whole" (Art. 4) and provides for jurisdiction in the EU court of the decedent's habitual residence. The applicable law (Art. 23) provides for the law of the decedent's domicile at death, but – as in other applicable law regulations – allows for that law's displacement by a "more closely connected" law. What is quite new is Article 22 (with at least one forerunner, in New York law), which permits the decedent to make a choice of law (apart from the Regulation's manifold alternatives for formal validity (Art. 27, see 4.6.2.3)), applicable to the substance of his or her dispositions. The choice is limited, however, to the substitution of the law of citizenship for that of the domicile at death. If the law chosen by the decedent is that of an EU Member State, the "parties concerned" may agree on the exclusive jurisdiction of the appropriate court of that Member State. A Member State court that has jurisdiction under the Regulation's general provision (decedent's habitual residence) may also decline jurisdiction at the heir's request on *forum non conveniens* grounds in favor of another Member State's court.

When there is a danger that the heirs may not pay (or be able to pay) the decedent's debts (as they are obliged to do under the civil law's rule of direct devolution on the heirs), the court may order "administration" of the estate (Art. 29), essentially placing the property under the control of an administrator. This is similar to the role of an American administrator of a decedent's estate, or of a trustee in bankruptcy. The difference with respect to an American administrator is, of course, that the latter deals only with the property under his or her particular jurisdiction, while the European counterpart deals with the estate as a whole.

4.6.2.5 Recognition

The procedural, but also some of the substantive, differences among legal systems may create problems in the context of international recognition. For instance, in a civil law succession case, against whom does a common law creditor bring his or her claim? Against the universal legatee, or against an American ancillary administrator in the state in which there are assets? In protecting a local claimant, an American court opted for the latter.[25] Consider the reverse: Would a civil law court honor a common law administrator's claim to property over that of a legatee when the applicable (substantive) law is its own?

Furthermore, what if, as was permissible at the time, the testator chose New York law for his testamentary disposition, thereby to preclude the widow's right to take against the will under the law of the testator's domicile? Here, New York protected the weaker party, disregarded the testator's choice, and applied the testator's domiciliary law.[26] In effect, the last example is a case of a court not only displacing the otherwise applicable law by reference to a mandatory norm of its own, but yielding to *another state's* mandatory rule (see 2.2.4, 4.2.1, 4.3.1.1, and 4.3.3.1).

Vexing questions can arise with respect to property rights. The common law knows many forms of "rights in property," in particular, the so-called "future interests," which permit the splitting of ownership in time, and not just possession as in a lease situation. Such interests may be transferred and held to be a part of the thing. For instance, title (ownership) may be transferred in a time sequence (for a number of years or for the transferee's lifetime, and the like), with title thereafter finally going to a designated person ("remainder") or "reverting" to the original grantor. Real property rights, moreover, can take the form of *rights to benefits*, again perhaps granted in different time sequences. These are property rights *in equity* and underlie the common law *trust*.

---

[25] *Lenn v. Richie*, 117 N.E.2d 129 (Mass. 1954).
[26] *Estate of Clark*, 236 N.E.2d 152 (N.Y. 1968). Citing Clark, a more modern decision adopted current state-interest-focussed choice of law (see 4.3.3.4–4.3.3.5): The applicable law is that of the state which has "the predominant interest." *In re Harvey*, 2012 WL 6761593, *2 (N.Y.Sur.Ct., November 30, 2012).

Many civil law systems follow the principle of a *numerus clausus* of property rights: There are only the rights established by law, no addition to them by party formulation is possible. What, then, is a civil law court to do when its conflicts law calls for the application of the law of the decedent's domicile at death, and the decedent's will provides for all kinds of future interest for named heirs, as is possible under his or her domiciliary law? The court cannot award rights unknown to its system. However, in order to honor the testator's intent (or a rule of the applicable law, for instance, a widow's common law life estate in the home (*dower*)), the court can approximate. Thus, the EU's Succession Regulation provides that the foreign right "be adapted to the closest right *in rem* of [the forum state], taking into account the aims and the interests pursued by the specific right *in rem* and the effects attached to it" (Art. 31). Within the EU, succession decisions of a Member State are recognized in the same manner, and subject only to the same limited defenses as other judgments in civil and commercial matters (see 5.5.1 and 5.5.2). In contrast to the applicable law ("universal application"), the recognition of judgments of non-EU states remains a matter for the national law of the Member States.

Similar problems can also arise in the reverse situation. For instance, legatees under a civil law "universal succession" (to the entire estate), in application, say, of the law of the decedent's domicile at death, seek recognition and enforcement of their inheritance by applying for registration of real estate in the situs state. If the latter is a common law jurisdiction, it will differentiate between movable and immovable property in inheritance cases. Therefore, situs law, and not the testator's domiciliary law, would apply to the succession to real estate. Assume that under situs law, the widow would have dower rights, but that under the testator's will (valid under domiciliary law), she gets no interest in the real property (but other things instead): Will the testamentary disposition or situs law override the respective other law? In such a case, "adaptation" (see previous paragraph) does not help; it is an either/or situation. There are American decisions applying situs law to determine the validity of a will with respect to local real estate. In such a case, it would depend on whether the situs regards the provision of dower rights (in the example) as "mandatory" (for mandatory rules, see 2.2.4 and 4.2.1) or subject to displacement by testamentary disposition. Given the social purpose for which dower rights exist, it is not implausible to argue that they cannot be displaced by the testator. In this case, a uniform result between systems would not have been achieved.

4.6.3 Corporate entities

Incorporated entities, whatever their names and forms, are "legal persons." What law applies to them, in the sense that "domicile" or "habitual residence" are applicable to natural persons for any number of issues (for instance, adjudicatory jurisdiction, or in family and succession law)? The EU Brussels Ia Regulation provides in its Article 63 that a corporation's statutory seat, place of central administration, or principal place of business is the equivalent of a natural person's domicile for purposes of *adjudicatory jurisdiction*, i.e., where it can be sued. Most legal systems would agree that at least the last two grounds justify the exercise of jurisdiction.

But the foregoing assumes that the entity in question in a given case in fact is a corporation, and has the attributes of one (for instance, limited liability). What law determines that? In common law countries – and increasingly in other countries as well – it is the law of an entity's state of incorporation that defines its status and usually also governs its internal affairs. The place of incorporation is the same as the "statutory seat" in the previous paragraph: It is the place of incorporation, registration, and the like, which, however, may have nothing to do with the corporation's center of management or activity. Thus, because of its attractive corporation law, many American companies are "Delaware companies," meaning that they were incorporated there, even though their business activity is centered entirely elsewhere. Two or three other American states are equally as attractive for incorporation as Delaware.

Some civil law countries, for instance Austria and Germany, use another connecting factor to determine the applicable law: It is the place of the entity's "seat," somewhat akin to the "place of central administration," which may or may not be the same as the other two possible locations (place of incorporation or principal place of business). Problems with the "seat theory" can result from a change of the entity's "real seat," for instance, when over time, one division or branch becomes more important than before and decision-making shifts to the new location, making it now the place of central management. At this point, the company may lose its corporate status (by deregistration) in the original state (having moved its seat elsewhere) and may not have complied with formal requirements, as it should have, in the state of its new seat. In such a case, it may now have lost its status – and with it, limited liability – in both states. The same result would follow if the second state were an "incorporation state," willing to recognize the foreign company's status:

having lost its corporate status in the first ("seat") state, there is nothing to recognize in the second state.

This difference in the basic approach is an obvious obstacle to the movement of companies and their cross-border manufacturing, sales, or service activities. In the EU, the Court of Justice therefore adopted the "incorporation theory" for the determination of the law applicable to corporations *within the EU*, with national law remaining in effect with respect to non-EU companies.[27] The German Supreme Court adopted this approach for purposes of the free movement of companies under the German–American Treaty of Friendship, Commerce, and Navigation.[28]

In the United States, which follows the "incorporation theory," confirmed by the United States Supreme Court as applicable to a corporation's internal affairs, at least one state (California) introduced its own limited version of the "seat theory." Companies, though incorporated elsewhere, but with a certain (high) percentage of Californian shareholders and a certain number of Californians on the managerial board, are termed "pseudo-foreign corporations" and subject to California law as if they were local companies. The law is limited to companies not traded on national stock exchanges, presumably to avoid imposing a burden on interstate commerce and thereby running afoul of the United States Supreme Court's jurisprudence. The highest court of the state of Delaware considers the California law to be unconstitutional and refused to give it effect in Delaware.[29] The issue has not yet been finally decided on the federal level.

---

27   Case C-212/97, *Centros Ltd v. Erhvervs- og Selskabsstyrelsen*, 1999 E.C.R. I-1459.
28   Bundesgerichtshof [BGH] [Federal Court of Justice], Jan. 29, 2003, VIII ZR 155/02, [2003] IPRax 265.
29   *Juul Labs, Inc. v. Grove*, 238 A.3d 904, 914-18 (Del. Ch. 2020); applied in *Diesenhouse v. Social Learning and Payments, Inc.*, 2022 WL 3100562, *10 (S.D.N.Y., August 3, 2022).

4.7 Forum policy: mandatory norms and the public policy exception

Previous discussions have touched upon the forum's strong policy concerns and its "governmental interests" in the resolution of an international conflicts situation. It was seen that the forum regulates a certain subject generally, and will not have that regulation displaced by party stipulation or by a choice-of-law rule. These are "mandatory rules," discussed above in the context of the EU Rome I Regulation (see 2.2.4 and 4.3.1.1.1). Such a rule expresses the forum's overriding policy generally, without regard to a specific case; in other words, before an international conflicts case even arises. When such a case does arise, there might be a question of whether the forum may or should impose its law in this fashion. In most cases, the forum will have sufficient contact with the case to make this reasonable; for other cases, suffice it to note that forum law and its potential mandatory application were known to or could have been found out by the parties beforehand.

The "public policy exception" deals with the individual case: Its outcome, through law stipulated by the parties or the result of a choice-of-law rule, is unpalatable to the forum. Dislike or disagreement with the result from the forum's perspective is not enough; the result must offend basic values of the forum. All conflicts systems impose such a high requirement before the otherwise applicable law may be rejected. The EU's judgment recognition law (see 5.5.4) even states expressly that the public policy exception may not be used as a subterfuge to question another state's jurisdiction to deny recognition to its judgment.

What happens if the forum's public policy fundamentally objects to the foreign law? The tendency will be simply to disregard the foreign rule at this point and to apply one's own law. But this is not a "false conflict" case, in which this would be the right automatic conclusion (see 4.3.3.1). By definition, a conflict exists in the present situation. Application of one's own law (exporting it) may impose or increase an obligation that is equally contrary to the otherwise applicable law, as discussed in the context of damages (see 4.5.1). Before applying its own law, this is a concern the forum should recognize and address. If the result would negatively impact a party, a better course would be to dismiss the case – not to entertain it at all ("I cannot do this") – leaving the party free to seek a remedy elsewhere.

4.8 How to determine the content of applicable foreign law?

4.8.1 How does foreign law become applicable?

A state's conflicts rules may provide that foreign law should apply to a particular case or issue.[30] How does foreign law enter into the court's consideration and decision? In civil law jurisdictions, all laws – the forum's own law as well as foreign law – are considered equal, although perhaps different in scope or limited in their applicability, territorially or otherwise. When the forum's conflicts law refers to a foreign law, it thereby makes a choice between two "laws." Deciding legal issues is the function of the judge (the court) in all systems. In the civil law, consideration and use of foreign law thus becomes part of the decision-making process *as a matter of law.*

In contrast, the (American) common law regards as "law" only that which emanates from or is pronounced by authority of the forum's sovereign. All else, such as foreign rules, is therefore *fact*, and facts must be brought before the court. If they are not, they will not be considered and the court's decision will be based on the only "law" it knows – forum law.

4.8.2 Determining the content of and applying foreign law

The foregoing already shows that in a civil law system it is the judge who determines that foreign law is applicable. He does this on the basis of the reference to it by the forum's (usually codified) conflicts law, and then determines the content of that law because, as stated, the foreign law is "law" and the ancient maxim states that *iura novit curia* (the court knows the law). But having to know all the world's laws is quite a daunting task; in practice, the court will therefore need help (see below).

---

[30] For a comprehensive country-by-country survey, see Yuko Nishitani (ed.), *Treatment of Foreign Law: Dynamics Towards Convergence?* (Vol. 26 of *Ius Comparatum* – Global Studies in Comparative Law) (Springer Verlag, 2017). For a detailed report on American law, see Peter Hay, "The United States: The Use and Determination of Foreign Law in Civil Litigation in the United States", in ibid. at 397–427, reprinted in 62 Am. J. Comp. L. Supp. 213 (2014).

In common law systems, it will be remembered, the parties (through their lawyers) conduct the case (the adversarial proceeding). They present their claims and all that supports them to the "trier of facts" – the judge or a jury. The judge supervises the proceeding, makes rulings of law, and instructs the jury at the request of the parties. The combination of how a common law proceeding is conducted and the view of foreign law as "fact" means that a party wishing to rely on a rule of foreign law must invoke it and then proceed to prove its content. The role of the judge is limited to the question of forum law: whether, under its conflicts law, the invocation of foreign law is appropriate. A party who fails to show the content of foreign law, therefore, has failed to meet its burden of proof and loses. Some presumptions ameliorate this result, but often are inapplicable: for instance, that the foreign law belongs to the common law family and therefore can be presumed to be the same as forum law, or that the foreign state involved is "uncivilized" so that forum law remains as the only appropriate law. Furthermore, because foreign law is "fact," a court cannot take judicial notice of it. Yet a further consequence is that the decision of the trier of facts, usually the jury, is not appealable. Thus, a jury of lay people will render an unappealable decision as to contents of foreign law, perhaps without even being able to read original texts in the foreign language. In civil law systems, in contrast, the court's determination, being one on a question of "law," is appealable.

In both systems, legal experts – academics, practitioners, including from an involved foreign state itself – will be called upon to assist. In the civil law, the court will appoint an individual expert or an academic research institution to provide it with *expertise* on the content of the foreign law with respect to the issue at hand. Parties may also be asked to assist the court. In the common law system, it will be the parties who will hire experts to advise them and, if their research seems promising, to prepare a memorandum in support of their position. An obvious worry (and critique of this system) is that a party's expert will not be objective but present a partisan conclusion – that he or she is no more than "a hired gun."

In some common law countries, for instance in the United States, but not to this extent in the United Kingdom, the fact approach has been modified. In American federal court practice, a party must still give notice of its intention to invoke foreign law (in retention of the fact-oriented adversarial approach) but must thereafter assist the *court* in its undertaking to determine the content of the foreign law. The court's determination will then be treated as one of an issue of law and is therefore appealable. As in earlier practice, party assistance will most often take the form of the tender of testimony or written statements by (party-retained) experts. But, as another departure from the earlier fact approach, which requires proof by the party, the court may also undertake its own research.

PART III

Judgments

5 Recognition and enforcement of foreign judgments

5.1 Introduction

Previous chapters discussed proceedings in State A from the perspective of how that state, under its law or under applicable international norms, acquires decision-making authority – "jurisdiction" – over the subject matter and over the parties in a dispute; and on what basis, using what methodology, it decides the controversy ("applicable law"). In a purely domestic (internal) case, and after possible appeals have been exhausted, this will end the matter: The same state authority that authorized and regulated the progress of the proceeding provides for the implementation ("enforcement") of its result.

Matters are far more difficult and involved in international cases, here defined as cases in which the determination in State A cannot be implemented in State A alone but requires some action in one or more other states. This may be the case when a defendant's assets in State A are insufficient to satisfy a State A money judgment, when implementation of a custody decree requires the return of the child from another state, or when a person owing support has now moved to another state, to give but a few examples.

These cases raise a number of important questions, most of which will be explored in the subsections that follow. They include, among others: What must be the nature of the State A action before its enforcement in State B can be sought – for instance, is a fee charged by a local library in State A collectible in State B? Will State B act as a tax collector for State

A, or enforce a penalty imposed in a State A criminal conviction? Can the debtor-defendant raise defenses against enforcement in State B (thereby perhaps starting the case all over again)? How automatic (or procedurally involved) is enforcement in State B? And, once recognized, does the State A decree (or whatever it is) have the same, less, or even more effect in State B than at home?

5.2 The nature of the foreign decree

5.2.1 Finality

Recognition in State B presupposes that what happened in State A *decided* something, that is, it was not a mere statement of opinion, policy, or the like. Rather, it *bound* the parties; it established rights and obligations. Many types of decrees may do so, but they may be only interim measures, pending the final resolution of the dispute. This occurs, for instance, when a defendant's assets are frozen during litigation on the main claim or when a *ne exeat* order forbids the removal of a child during a custody dispute. It may also be that a decree, particularly one for support, is modifiable retroactively, so that recognition of State A's decree in State B becomes modifiable upon modification in State A.

For reasons of judicial economy, most legal systems traditionally required that the foreign decree be *final* before a request for local recognition and enforcement would be entertained. In the case of the retroactively modifiable support decree, this meant that the unpaid sum would first have to be reduced to a final judgment in State A. Interim orders, such as protective measures, might also not be enforced.

The requirement of finality has been relaxed in many systems. In the EU, for instance, the Brussels Ia Regulation expressly provides for the recognition of provisional methods (so long as adequate notice has been given: see 5.5.3). Finality of support decrees is no longer required in the United States. *Ne exeat* obligations (established by an order not to leave the country with the child during the pendency of the custody proceeding) are regarded as part of "custody rights" and thus enforceable under the Hague Convention (see 3.6.4). This relaxation perhaps increases burdens on the State B courts in our examples, but the resulting judicial cooperation makes it easier for a party to resolve the controversy in one, rather than in a series of proceedings.

Note, however, that the above addresses non-final, especially interim, measures of State A that are sought to be recognized in State B. If, in contrast, interim measures are sought in State B when litigation is pending in State A, the actions in State B may indeed impinge on a resolution in State A: They constitute an example of attempts to "race to judgment," discussed earlier (see 3.7.1), and should be dealt with under applicable *lis alibi pendens* provisions.

5.2.2   The issuing authority

States employ different tribunals, bodies, or agencies for the settlement of private civil and commercial disputes; the decision-maker is not always a "court," as it might be in the recognizing state, nor is the decision always called a "judgment." For convenience, this part of the book uses the term "recognition and enforcement of judgments." But "judgment" in the present context does not carry the possibly narrow meaning of "judgment by a court." The name of the decision-maker and how its decision is styled are not important. It is rather the binding effect on the parties, as defined by the law of the issuing state, that characterizes something as a "judgment" for purposes of the present discussion. To illustrate: the Supreme Court of New South Wales recognized a Chinese "Judicial Mediation Settlement" as constituting a "judgment" under the Australian Uniform Civil Procedure Rules because such a mediation settlement, supervised by a judge, was enforceable in the People's Republic without further judicial proceedings and modifiable only by a court upon appeal.[1]

The following does exclude arbitration decisions, because their recognition internationally is governed by the 1958 New York Convention on the Recognition and Enforcement of Foreign Arbitral Awards,[2] which is in force in 169 countries, the Cook Islands, the Holy See, and the State of Palestine (as of 2022), and by the Convention on the Settlement of Investment Disputes between States and Nationals of Other States (the ICSID Convention), with 158 contracting states (as of 2022).

---

[1]   *Bank of China Ltd. v. Chen* (2022) NSWSC 749.
[2]   June 10, 1958, 21 U.S.T. 2517, 330 U.N.T.S. 38.

5.2.3   Effect in another state

A judgment has no force outside of the country in which it was rendered; that is how far the power of a local (rendering) court extends. It may *affect* persons outside of the state of rendition, for instance when a judgment awards title to local real property to a plaintiff as against a foreigner who so far had been the property's registered owner. This effect, however, does not result from the court's power over the foreign party (unless that party participated in the litigation), but from its power over the real property. In awarding title to the property to the plaintiff, the court acts on the property but does not adjudicate rights and obligations as between the parties. For that, the court would need personal jurisdiction over the foreign party.

To illustrate: A in State A holds a mortgage on B's house in State B. There is a dispute whether the mortgage has been paid off or whether B still owes money. To settle the matter, B brings an action in State B to have title to the house established in his name, free and clear of the mortgage; A does not participate. Assume that the State B court agrees with B and establishes clear title in B. What is the effect on A? He has lost the security interest in B's house that the mortgage gave him. But has he also lost his claim that B owes him money – a claim that so far had been secured by the mortgage? No. The B court had jurisdiction over the mortgage as it related to the local real property. To affect the personal obligations of the parties, it needed personal jurisdiction over both parties. It did not have that. Therefore, wherever A can get personal jurisdiction over B, he can still bring his claim that B owes him money, and if successful, he would get a money judgment in the amount of the debt, but not the real property *unless* the action were in a State B court (with jurisdiction over the property as well as the parties). (For additional discussion, see 5.6.)

Assume, in the foregoing example, that A recovers a money judgment, say in State C, for that which he claimed B owed him, but that B has no assets in C, whereas he does in State B. Can A take his C judgment to State B and have the appropriate official or authority there seize B's property, sell it, if necessary, and pay A the amount necessary to satisfy the C judgment? Again: no. The C judgment cannot reach assets outside of State C; it can only bind the parties (establish whether and how much one party owes the other). To get his C judgment satisfied, A must first get it recognized and then enforced wherever he tries to reach B's assets (in the example, in State B).

5.3   Methods of recognition – international solutions

5.3.1   Treaties

Countries can agree, by bilateral treaty with each other, on the reciprocal recognition of their judgments and the conditions that a judgment
must meet to benefit from the arrangements. Several countries maintain
a number of bilateral arrangements, for instance Russia and Turkey;
others do so only with respect to a few other countries, for instance China
with Bulgaria and Vietnam. In still others, such as France and Germany,
many former bilateral arrangements have now been replaced by the comprehensive EU legislation (see 4.1.2, 5.2.1, and 5.3.3), so that for Germany,
only its arrangement with Tunisia still remains.

The 2019 Hague Convention on the Recognition and Enforcement of
Foreign Judgments in Civil and Commercial Matters[3] replaced an earlier
version which had received only five ratifications.[4] The European Union
has acceded to it on behalf of 26 of its Member States, and Ukraine has
ratified it. So far Costa Rica, Israel, Russia, the United States, and Uruguay
have signed but not yet ratified the Convention. It will enter into force
on September 1, 2023. Intended for wide international acceptance, the
Convention is, of course, more limited in scope than, for instance, EU
jurisdiction and judgment-recognition law. It provides for the recognition and enforcement of "eligible" judgments and lists both the kinds of
judgments included and those not covered by it. Specific provisions deal
with choice-of-court clauses underlying a judgment, the jurisdiction of
courts at the place of performance of a contract, the place of conduct in
tort cases, and with consumers and employees. The long list of judgments
not covered includes judgments relating to maintenance, matrimonial
property and other family obligations, succession, defamation, privacy,
and arbitration. It will be noted that some of the foregoing are covered by
other international agreements (for instance, arbitration) or regional law
(such as the EU Succession Regulation). In addition, states may exclude
specific subjects or procedures by filing reservations when they deposit
their accession or ratification. Article 29 (the "bilateralization clause")

For the full text, see: https://www.hcch.net/en/instruments/conventions/full
     -text/?cid=137 (last visited November 7, 2022).

February 1, 1971, 1144 U.N.T.S. 249.

also permits states to declare that judgments of specified countries will not be recognized.

5.3.2   Reciprocal recognition arrangements

Some countries have, by domestic legislation or as part of a multilateral treaty, made arrangements for reciprocal judgment recognition. An example of the latter is the Protocol on Cooperation of the Latin American MERCOSUR group,[5] addressing judgment recognition among Brazil, Paraguay, and Uruguay. Comprehensive domestic legislation, for instance in Australia, the Russian Federation, Singapore, and the United Kingdom, extends reciprocal recognition mechanisms to a list of named countries. The Australian Foreign Judgments Act,[6] for example, includes the United Kingdom, Hong Kong, Japan, South Korea, Germany, France, and several Canadian provinces. The Russian Multilateral Convention of the Commonwealth of Independent States (1993)[7] provides for mutual assistance among countries formerly part of the Soviet Union. Singapore's Reciprocal Enforcement of Commonwealth Judgments Act (RECJA)[8] extends recognition to some ten countries.

The United States is not listed in any of these reciprocal recognition statutes, nor is it a member of bilateral recognition treaties. It maintains treaties of "Friendship, Commerce and Navigation" or of "Establishment" with many countries, but judgment recognition is not covered. One example is the United States–German treaty of 1954.[9] It provides in its Article VI(1) that nationals and companies of either country shall enjoy, in the territory of the other "national treatment with respect to access to the courts …, both in pursuit and defense of their rights …" Access is, of course, not yet recognition of judgments, and the latter is needed for any enforcement. As mentioned above, the United States has signed the

---

[5]   MERCOSUR Protocol on Jurisdictional Cooperation and Assistance in Civil, Commercial, Labor, and Administrative Matters, Dec. 5, 1992.

[6]   Foreign Judgments Act 1991 (Cth) (Austl.).

[7]   Agreement Establishing the Commonwealth of Independent States, 31 I.L.M. 142 (1992).

[8]   Reciprocal Enforcement of Foreign Judgments Act, Mar. 26, 1959, available at: https://statutes.agc.gov.sg/Act/REFJA1959 (accessed March 6, 2018).

[9]   Treaty of Friendship, Commerce and Navigation between the United States of America and the Federal Republic of Germany, Oct. 29, 1954, 7 U.S.T. 1839, 273 U.N.T.S. 3.

2019 Hague Convention on the Recognition and Enforcement of Foreign Judgments but has not yet ratified it.

5.3.3   The EU's "federal-type" approach

EU law was likened in previous contexts to legislation in a federal governmental structure, in that central law-making prevails over the laws of the constituent governmental units, except that these are not provinces, departments, or states as in the United States, but sovereign countries. The EU's founding instruments bestow law-making power on the Union's institutions in a number of substantive areas, including procedural law for border-crossing litigation within the Union. The EU's law on jurisdiction of courts and on choice of law in contract, tort, and succession were treated earlier (see 3.2, 3.3, and 4.3.1.1, respectively). EU law likewise provides for the effect to be given to a national EU court's judgment in other EU Member States.

EU law deals with the recognition and enforcement of Member States' judgments in civil and commercial law (Brussels Ia Regulation), in divorce and child custody (Brussels II*ter* Regulation), in succession, in insolvency, and in a number of additional, more specialized areas (such as small claims, the European Payment Order, and judgments with respect to uncontested claims). The recognition provisions – naturally, with some variations – are basically the same: The first state's judgment is to be recognized and enforced like a local judgment and to be given the same effect as in the state of rendition. The defenses available to the judgment debtor and the procedures for enforcement are far more judgment-creditor-friendly than any currently found in international treaties or in national legal systems.

The second state's court of first instance – for example, in cases falling under the Brussels Ia Regulation – is bound to enforce the first state's judgment without review. Defenses must be raised on appeal, and the appellate court may entertain only a defense based on a violation of the enforcing state's public policy, lack of proper notice to the judgment debtor of the pendency of the action in the first court, or the presence of inconsistent judgments. Note, in particular, that this list of permitted defenses does not include a claim that the issuing court lacked jurisdiction over the defendant. (For further discussion and limited exceptions, see 5.5.2.)

5.3.4   The Lugano Convention

When the EU's predecessor organization (the European Common Market, later the European Economic Community (EEC)) was formed, non-participating countries formed the European Free Trade Association (EFTA), which eliminated trade barriers within the area, but did not have a unified policy with respect to the outside world. Over time, many EFTA countries joined the EEC (now the EU), as did several Central and Eastern European countries that had not even been EFTA members. Today, EFTA comprises Iceland, Liechtenstein, Norway, and Switzerland. EFTA countries, then and now, have maintained close economic relations with the EU. An agreement between three EFTA countries (Iceland, Liechtenstein, and Norway) and the EU establishes the "European Economic Area" (EEA, the "internal market"), within which the EU's policies regarding free trade and movement of companies and persons apply.

Just as realization of the substantive law and policy of the EU required harmonization of procedural and conflicts law for the adjudication of cross-border disputes, the relationship between the EU and EFTA required the same. The result was the Lugano Convention of 2007 on jurisdiction and the recognition and enforcement of judgments, in force since 2010 among the EU, the EFTA states, and Denmark (which had opted out of the EU's Brussels I Regulation: see 4.1.2). In most important respects, the Lugano Convention replicates the Brussels I Regulation, but has not (yet) been revised in light of the Brussels Ia Regulation, in force since 2015. Some differences therefore exist. For instance, the Lugano Convention's jurisdictional provision protecting consumers is somewhat narrower than its Brussels Ia counterpart, and in judgment recognition, the Convention is still somewhat more traditional in its procedural provisions than the new Brussels Ia Regulation (with respect to the *exequatur*, see 5.4.1). With its withdrawal from the European Union ("Brexit"), the United Kingdom also ceased to be a member of the Lugano Convention and the EEA. It sought to accede to the Lugano Convention, but the European Union denied its required approval. It thus no longer enjoys the internal market arrangement of the EEA with Switzerland.

5.4   Methods of recognition – national law approaches

5.4.1   The civil law *exequatur*

Since judgment recognition as between two countries, except in the EU, very often will not be covered or assured by international agreements or as part of statutes granting reciprocal recognition, the receiving country's national law (statutory or common law) determines recognition and enforcement of any particular foreign judgment. Such a judgment, as noted earlier, needs recognition to be enforced; it carries no authority of its own. In fact, it is technically only a foreign act, and not a "judgment," because it was not rendered under the authority of the recognizing state. Such a view of a foreign "judgment" has two consequences.

First, it must obviously be recognized before it can be enforced. In civil law countries, traditionally recognition has been achieved by the judgment creditor applying for a certificate of enforceability, the so-called "*exequatur*." Thus authorized by the local court, local officials could then enforce the judgment, for instance, by seizing the judgment debtor's assets.

Second, the *exequatur* only authorizes the enforcement of the foreign judgment; it does not thereby become a new judgment of the recognizing state. Why is this important? Consider a judgment rendered by a court in State A. The judgment creditor now seeks its enforcement in State B, and for that purpose, obtains an *exequatur*. It now appears that the judgment debtor's assets in State B are insufficient, so the creditor needs to look for additional assets, for instance in State C. Will State C authorize enforcement of the State A judgment against local assets (in State C) on the basis of the State B *exequatur*? No. State B only authorized enforcement in State B (for instance, because State B's preconditions for recognition were satisfied); it did not purport to give the State A judgment the same status that a judgment of its own courts would have. The *exequatur* thus is not a State B judgment, enforcement of which could be sought in State C. Instead, the judgment creditor must seek recognition and enforcement of the original State A judgment all over again in State C, and is thereby subject to any defenses that the debtor would have under State C law against a State A judgment (which might be different from defenses against a State B judgment).

The recast of the EU's Brussels I Regulation (i.e., the current Brussels Ia Regulation) now provides in its Article 39 that a Member State judgment "shall be enforceable ... without any declaration of enforceability being required." The need for an *exequatur* has been abolished within the EU. It is still required by and in relation to countries of the Lugano Convention. Nor does the change in the Brussels Ia Regulation affect the conclusion to the hypothetical case in the preceding paragraph: If State A is an EU country, no *exequatur* is needed; if it is a non-EU country, recognition by one EU country – for instance, State B – will not turn it into a State B *judgment* (but see 5.4.2 for the common law).

In countries (outside the EU) that continue to require an *exequatur*, its grant – in addition to other defenses against the recognition of the foreign judgment (see 5.5) – will often depend on "reciprocity," meaning that the country that rendered the judgment would recognize the second state's judgment in like circumstances. The next subsection elaborates further on this.

5.4.2 Recognition under common law

Several common law countries have statutes providing for the reciprocal recognition of judgments of particular countries, as described earlier. For judgments that do not benefit from such a specific reciprocal recognition statute, recognition must be sought under the traditional common law approach.

The famous United States Supreme Court decision in *Hilton v. Guyot*[10] explored at great length, much of it really *obiter dicta* (that is, observations not necessary for the decision of the case before the Court), why and under what circumstances an American court would recognize a foreign judgment. Such a judgment, after all, is not a "judgment" by local standards, as stated above. It is really only a "fact." That fact represents the "judgment" creditor's *claim*, upon which a local suit is brought. If and when successful, a local judgment (a *real* judgment, as it were) would be granted on that claim. As a local judgment, it is then, of course, enforceable.

The foreign "judgment" will be recognized and transformed into an enforceable local judgment on the basis of "comity," so said the Supreme

---

[10]   159 U.S. 113 (1895).

Court. "Comity," an elusive concept, is neither an obligation under international law nor a simple expression of good feelings. It is not a matter of whim. It expresses the desire, through courtesy and respect for the other state, to promote and facilitate living and functioning together as an international community. But this cooperative spirit has limits; it presupposes a like cooperative spirit on the other side. This means that judgment recognition on the basis of comity is granted on the basis of *reciprocity*. If reciprocity is lacking, the foreign judgment will continue to be regarded as a mere claim, to be reviewed by the recognizing court on the merits, including the procedure and the law on which the foreign court based its judgment. This is the so-called *révision au fond*, looking behind the foreign judgment. The decision in the *Hilton* case was actually much narrower than its sweeping language suggested: The French judgment in favor of a French plaintiff against an American was denied recognition because French courts, in the reverse situation, would re-examine an American judgment. The *Hilton* court indicated that a French judgment *in favor* of an American would not be refused recognition, nor would decisions relating to family status (e.g., divorce).

The reciprocity requirement has been dropped in all but a few states of the United States (foreign judgment recognition now being a matter of state, and not of federal, law). Foreign-country judgments are generally recognized almost like sister-state judgments. Likewise, when this is the case, there generally is no *révision au fond* (some differences with respect to both are noted at 5.5.5.2 and 5.5.5.3). In the EU, with its mandate of recognition of judgments of EU countries' national courts, reciprocity is, of course, not an issue, and any review of another Member State's judgment on the merits ("substance," meaning *révision au fond*) is expressly forbidden.

5.4.2.1 *Recognition within the United States*

In the United States, there is a difference between the recognition of a sister-state judgment and a judgment by a court of a foreign country. With most areas and issues of private law being the law of the individual states, a sister-state judgment is technically a "foreign" judgment. However, the relationship of the various states to one another is a federal matter (for instance, the delineation of state lines, i.e., borders). So is the effect of one state's judgment in another, and the Federal Constitution expressly mandates interstate recognition in its "Full Faith and Credit"

Clause (Article IV). Its implementing statute further defines what full faith and credit means: A state is to give sister-state judgments the same effect that they have in the state "from which they are taken."

The Full Faith and Credit Clause does not change the *manner* in which the judgment creditor gets his or her judgment recognized and enforced in another state. In the common law tradition, the first judgment is still a claim upon which the creditor must bring a suit to obtain a local judgment, which can then be enforced against the debtor's assets. What the constitutional clause does effect is that a local judgment *must* issue so long as the creditor presents a valid judgment of a sister state. For available defenses, see 5.5.

Bringing suit on a sister-state judgment costs time. In states with heavy dockets, assets may be dissipated or removed while the recognition and enforcement action is pending. If the judgment is one for money or property and was rendered by a federal court, federal law permits it to be registered in any other federal court. A state court judgment, however, is still subject to the common law method, as described. To reduce this burden, a number of states have adopted uniform legislation for similar registration of sister-state judgments. Another uniform law expedites the recognition and enforcement of foreign-country judgments.

In the interstate setting, a judgment creditor thus may have a choice between recognition by suit (the common law way) or recognition under the uniform act. Choosing the former subjects the creditor only to defenses available in the state of rendition (viz. same effect as where rendered), while using the uniform act also subjects him or her to local defenses available in the state of recognition. This exposure to the additional defenses is the price the judgment creditor pays for speed.

5.5   Defenses to recognition and enforcement

5.5.1   In general

All legal systems allow a judgment debtor to interpose defenses against the recognition and enforcement of another state's judgment. This is true even when recognition is mandated, such as in the United States for interstate judgments and in the EU for Member State judgments. In all cases, the judgment must, first of all, be a "valid" judgment – but by whose standards? Furthermore, the judgment must not be subject to defenses in either the state of rendition or the state of recognition. Some common defenses to recognition include that the statute of limitations has run, that there is another, conflicting, judgment, or that in the state of recognition, recognizing the judgment would violate its public policy.

The more integrated legal systems are – the prime examples, once again, being the United States and the EU – the fewer the defenses that individual units can assert. As such, there will be a difference between inter-system judgments and those involving outside ("truly foreign") states. In this light, a first defense that might be considered in the latter situation is the claim that the judgment sought to be recognized is not valid because the rendering court lacked jurisdiction. It will be recalled (see 1.2.4) that "jurisdiction" really has two aspects: the jurisdiction (power to adjudicate) that is conferred upon a court by its own law, and the acceptance of that assertion by a second (recognizing) state, i.e., "jurisdiction in the international sense." These two aspects may create a situation in which a state has jurisdiction under its own law, but the second state will not accept it because it regards such jurisdiction as "exorbitant."

5.5.2   Lack of jurisdiction

5.5.2.1   Unified systems – the United States and the EU

In a unified system, judgment recognition also presupposes that the rendering court had proper jurisdiction. However, the standard for testing the rendering court's jurisdiction will not be defined by the system's component (an individual state in the United States, a Member State in the EU), but centrally. In the EU, the Brussels Ia Regulation specifies the permissible bases of jurisdiction that may be asserted against a Member State defendant. As was seen earlier (see 3.2.1), all other bases that might be available under national law are excluded as "exorbitant." The same is true of the Lugano Convention. With regard to non-Member State defendants, an EU national court still uses its forum's standards (see 3.2.1, 5.5.2.2).

In the United States, the individual states define the reach of their jurisdiction (for instance, by way of "long-arm" statutes, just as the United Kingdom specifies the circumstances justifying service out of the jurisdiction), but there is a federal limit: the Due Process Clause of the Federal Constitution, under which the United States Supreme Court defines the outer limits of state court jurisdiction. With jurisdiction seen as part of due process, an American state court also may not recognize a foreign-country judgment that exceeds American due process limits.

There is a major difference between the United States and the EU with respect to how the defendant raises the defense that the rendering court lacked jurisdiction. The United States uses the traditional approach, generally followed by all legal systems: The defendant may raise the defense in the original *or* in the recognition proceeding, and challenge an adverse ruling by appeal, ultimately seeking United States Supreme Court review. In the EU, in contrast, the recognizing court may not review the first court's jurisdiction. Objections to that court's jurisdiction (except in specified cases protecting weaker parties) must be raised in that court, and appeals, if necessary, must be taken in that Member State. Ultimate review is by the EU Court of Justice. The EU system thus is much stricter than that of the United States: It forces the defendant to litigate jurisdiction in the first court, and does not give him or her the choice, as in United States law, to stay out of the first proceeding (default) and later to raise lack of jurisdiction as a defense against recognition of the default judgment in the second state. This may seem burdensome but must be seen in the context of the strict, defendant-protective provision of EU law requiring actual notice to the defendant in time to prepare a defense.

5.5.2.2 Testing another country's jurisdiction under national law

When no superior norm defines jurisdiction, on what basis does a recognizing court determine whether the rendering state had "jurisdiction in the international sense," i.e., jurisdiction that it, the second state, is willing to accept as adequate?

In defining and in asserting for jurisdiction itself, a state establishes rules that it considers fair or that appear to be necessary to protect interests of local parties. But what seems necessary to protect a rendering state's interests may be regarded as unfair by a recognizing state. "Exorbitant" rules of jurisdiction are examples of the latter. For this reason, a recognizing state will judge a rendering state's jurisdiction by its own (local) standards – the "mirror image" approach. For example, an English court may recognize an American judgment based on "transient service" (instituting suit by serving the defendant while present locally, even if only casually and temporarily: see 3.2.1). It will not regard assertion of jurisdiction by the first state as "exorbitant" and unacceptable, because the English system itself utilizes this method for exercising jurisdiction. The same American judgment would not be recognized by a German court. Its system requires a closer connection of the defendant and the dispute with Germany than mere casual presence of the defendant when the suit is started. Jurisdiction based on transient service is unacceptable by these standards; the requirement that the foreign assertion of jurisdiction be a "mirror image" of what one would do oneself has not been met. In reverse, an American court would not recognize a German judgment when the rendering court did not have personal jurisdiction over the judgment debtor but asserted jurisdiction because the latter had property in Germany when that property was unrelated to the claim. The mere presence of property suffices when the claim relates to it (*in rem* jurisdiction), but not when it only served to support jurisdiction for other (unrelated) claims (see 3.1 and 3.2). The use of *in rem* jurisdiction for claims requiring personal jurisdiction would be regarded as exorbitant.

Insistence on the foreign law being an exact "mirror image" of one's own would seem to go too far. At the bottom of the inquiry is the forum's concern that its own standards of fairness are not undercut by the foreign court's assertion of jurisdiction. "Mirror image" is too mechanical a test for fairness. Consider this example: An Austrian court asserts jurisdiction over an American on the basis of his having an Austrian bank account unrelated to the claim. All necessary papers instituting suit were served on him by the Austrian public authority while he was vacationing in Vienna. He did not appear, a default judgment issued, and recognition and enforcement is now sought in the United States. Jurisdiction on the basis of the defendant's ownership of claim-unrelated property in a state is improper under American law.[11] Application of a "mirror image" approach would require denial of the request for recognition and enforcement. But was the exercise of jurisdiction by Austria really unfair? After all, the defendant was served while in Austria, and the exercise of transient jurisdiction is permissible under American law. Rather than insisting on an exact, literal, "mirror image," a preferable approach for testing the fairness of the exercise of jurisdiction by the foreign court

---

[11]   See preceding paragraph. Earlier contrary American law was held to be unconstitutional in *Shaffer v. Heitner*, 433 U.S. 186 (1977).

RECOGNITION AND ENFORCEMENT OF FOREIGN JUDGMENTS 125

would be to ask whether the forum would have exercised jurisdiction on the same facts in the reverse situation.

5.5.3 Notice

"Service," as discussed earlier (see 3.9), takes different forms in different legal systems, from service on the defendant by the plaintiff directly, to service on the defendant by public authority, or even service *on* the public authority (*remise au parquet*). One of its functions is to fix the date when the action commences. That date starts the procedural calendar – for instance, within how many days after commencement of the action must the defendant file an answer? Within what time limit must the plaintiff then reply to it? What kinds of motions or requests for interim measures are permissible, and when must they be raised? At the same time, service will usually give the defendant notice of the suit, but that is not always the case. Although papers have been filed with the court, they may not reach the defendant for any number of reasons.

Fairness to the defendant, as discussed in the preceding subsection, requires not only that he or she was properly subject to the jurisdiction of the rendering court, but that he or she had notice of the suit and thereby an opportunity to defend against it. One might say that jurisdiction (by the standards of both the court of rendition and the court of recognition) is the *basis* for its exercise by the court of rendition, and that notice to the defendant is needed to *perfect it*.

What kind of notice? In a case dealing with the question of when notice by publication (e.g., in a newspaper) might be acceptable, the United States Supreme Court gave no definite rules, but emphasized that the burden to give the defendant notice is on the plaintiff. He or she must utilize the best method available to someone "desirous of actually informing the absentee."[12] Notice is a due process requirement. As a practical matter, notice by publication is permissible only when the defendant's address is unknown and cannot be ascertained with reasonable effort.

EU law is more direct in stating the need for notice. This is because a Member State judgment may not be recognized when the defendant did not receive notice in time to prepare a defense. "Pro forma" notice

---

[12]   *Mullane v. Cent. Hanover Bank & Trust Co.*, 339 U.S. 306, 315 (1950).

thus does not suffice; it must provide sufficient opportunity (for instance, sufficient time, but also sufficient detail) to make the preparation of a full defense possible. Read literally, EU law does not permit substituted service, for instance by publication, as discussed above for United States law, because an opportunity for the defendant to prepare a defense is not assured. National law, of course, continues in effect concerning methods of substituted service on non-EU defendants.

5.5.4 Conflicting judgments

A court may be faced with two (or even more) judgments – involving the same parties and the same cause of action – that are inconsistent or perhaps even contradictory. They may have been issued by courts of other countries, or a foreign judgment may be inconsistent with a judgment of the present court's own country. Assuming that all judgments are otherwise valid (i.e., rendered by a court with proper jurisdiction and with sufficient notice to all parties), which judgment shall the court enforce? (See also 3.7.1 with respect to the "race to judgment" and *lis pendens*.)

One way to deal with this problem is to consider the time sequence and make the decision turn on that. But which judgment carries the greater weight – the earlier one or the later one? Here, American practice is quite contrary to that of most other countries, in particular to that of the EU.

In American practice, the assumption is that the earlier-in-time judgment was before the second court. That court, in going ahead and entering its own inconsistent judgment, must therefore have considered the earlier judgment to be defective in some respect, for instance by concluding, however incorrectly, that the first court lacked jurisdiction. That the first judgment is not entitled to recognition is thus necessarily a part of the second court's decision and is *res judicata* as between the parties. (See 5.6.1 for what American courts consider to be *res judicata*.) As a result, the later judgment (the second one) is entitled to recognition and enforcement. Because this result follows from the *res judicata* effect of the last-in-time judgment, this rule applies regardless of whether the first of the inconsistent judgments was one rendered by a foreign court or by a court of the forum state.

The opposite result obtains in the EU and other countries with respect to inconsistent judgments rendered by foreign courts (for an inconsistent domestic judgment, see below). In these countries, effect is given to the judgment that was first in time. The second (later) judgment is not considered. One explanation might be that when the first judgment was rendered, nothing remained for a later court to consider and to decide. But what about the later court's implicit rejection of the earlier judgment? Again, a different view of what constitutes *res judicata* (see 5.6.1) may explain: Only what was actually litigated becomes *res judicata* in civil law countries. The "implicit rejection" (of the previous sentence and previous paragraph) does not count; the first court decided the merits, and its decision was not challenged on appeal (or an appeal failed), and therefore became final.

However, EU law is not consistent in its approach when inconsistent judgments before the court include one that was rendered by a court of the forum state. American courts apply their rule across the board; EU law gives preference to a local (domestic) inconsistent judgment, regardless of whether it was the earlier or the later judgment. This result, adopted in all EU Regulations relating to the recognition of Member State decisions, could be explained before January 2015 (when the Brussels Ia Regulation became applicable) by the fact that another state's judgment needed a certificate of enforceability (*exequatur*: see 5.4.1) to be entitled to enforcement in the forum state, while a local judgment, wherever rendered, had that effect immediately. This does not seem to be a good reason: All countries, including the United States (which follows a different rule, as discussed above), do not give immediate effect to a foreign judgment, but have procedures for its recognition. Furthermore, the *exequatur* was abolished within the EU by the Brussels Ia Regulation, but the latter continues to state the same forum-judgment-favoring rule.

The EU rule (Brussels Ia, Art. 45(1)(c) and (d)) expresses a public policy in favor of the forum (recognizing) state's judgment; considerations of time sequence do not apply. Similarly, and again as an obvious expression of public policy, a Member State judgment must be refused recognition if it conflicts with the jurisdictional provisions protecting weaker parties (insureds, insurance beneficiaries, consumers, employees: see 3.3.3; Brussels Ia, Art. 45(1)(a) and (e)). An important further provision of Article 45 (noted earlier: see 5.5.2) is its subsection (3), which provides that the jurisdiction of the first court may not be reviewed by the second court in all other cases, and that the general public policy defense of Article 45(1)(a) may not be used to circumvent this prohibition. This provision shows that the undercurrents of public policy also underlie the refusal-of-recognition provisions, including the rules on inconsistent judgments.

5.5.5   Public policy

5.5.5.1   *In general*

All legal systems refuse to recognize a foreign judgment that violates the forum state's public policy. That sounds obvious, but what is a state's public policy that its courts will, indeed must, protect against a foreign judgment that would violate it? The famous American judge, later Supreme Court Justice Cardozo, emphasized how limited the use of the public policy defense should be. In a much-quoted passage from 1918, he wrote: "The courts are not free to refuse to enforce a foreign right at the pleasure of the judges ... They do not close their doors, unless help would violate some fundamental principle of justice, some prevalent conception of good morals, some deep-rooted tradition of the common weal."[13] The message is clear: Personal dislikes do not rise to the level of public policy. But when does a foreign judgment so fundamentally offend our sense of justice that it should not be recognized? Surely, when the foreign judgment requires the doing of an act that would violate the forum's law, as standards of conduct cannot be imposed.

A corollary is that the forum court also will not be the enforcer of punishment imposed by a foreign court for the violation of that country's standards of conduct. "The courts of no country execute the penal laws of another."[14] Today, this statement may be overly broad and the question may be more nuanced: Does the foreign state benefit from the penalty, or does an individual? In the United States' interstate setting, for instance, a judgment for punitive damages may be recognized by another state if the award goes to the plaintiff, but not if it (or part of it) goes to the other state. The same American judgment for punitive damages, however, would be denied recognition in Germany. In the view of its courts, all forms of punishment are matters that belong to criminal law, thus they are subject to the rules of criminal procedure, including its defenses, and are not properly part of a civil case.

---

[13]   *Loucks v. Standard Oil Co. of New York*, 120 N.E. 198, 202 (N.Y. 1918).
[14]   *The Antelope*, 23 U.S. (10 Wheat.) 66, 123 (1825).

The forum's public policy also appears in other forms, which are often not articulated as such. Reciprocity, as a condition of judgment recognition (see 5.4.2), is the forum state's way to retaliate when the state rendering the judgment does not practice ready recognition of an otherwise valid judgment from the forum. However, this burdens the judgment creditor, who thus may not get his or her judgment recognized, but does not directly hurt the rendering state (unless the judgment creditor is one of its own citizens). Therefore, such practice is unlikely to prompt the rendering state to change its policy. What a strict reciprocity requirement does is present an obstacle to the free flow of judgments, with whatever effects that obstacle may have on commerce and investments.

Earlier discussion of the choice of the applicable law also encountered a forum's public policy, which might reject an otherwise applicable law. "Mandatory rules" of local law (requiring application without regard to what other law might otherwise be applicable) also reject foreign law (see 2.2.4, 4.3.1.1.1). The difference is that a rejection on articulated public policy grounds occurs after the foreign law has been determined to be otherwise applicable, while resort to the forum's mandatory rules does not even inquire whether a law other than the forum's might be applicable. The existence of mandatory rules (as an expression of the forum's public policy) also means, in the present context, that when a recognizing court engages in *révision au fond* (see 5.5.5.2 and 5.5.5.3), and the rendering court has ignored a mandatory norm of the recognizing court's state, the foreign judgment will not be recognized.[15]

5.5.5.2 *Public policy and révision au fond*

In the situations discussed above, it was fairly easy to see why a court would deny recognition for violation of its state's public policy. But how is it possible to make an assessment when the possible public policy violation does not appear on the face of the foreign judgment? Take, for instance, a foreign judgment for money, when the underlying debt resulted from a gambling contract, and gambling is forbidden in the state

---

[15] A good example is the careful decision in *Sicre de Fontbrune v. Wofsy*, 39 F.4th 1214 (9th Cir. 2022) in which the court concluded that a French judgment, on its facts, was not inconsistent with American law and therefore did not violate the forum's public policy. Note that the court engaged in a *révision au fond* to reach this conclusion. See also 5.4.2 and 5.5.5.2.

where recognition is sought. The answer is easy in the United States in the *interstate context.*

The common law rule is that the underlying cause of action merges in the judgment (here, the claim arising from the gambling contract). The claim is now gone, and what remains is the judgment; it is for money, and a judgment for money cannot offend the local public policy. The answer may be different when the American court is asked to enforce a foreign-country judgment, for instance, if the judgment in the foregoing gambling case had been rendered in Mexico. Here, the rule (much criticized in the literature[16]) is that the judgment does *not* merge the cause of action – it is still "visible," as it were, and thus may be offensive to the recognizing forum.

Matters become still more complicated when one wonders how all this can mesh with the abandonment of *révision au fond.* That doctrine, it will be recalled (see 5.4.2), led to a re-examination of a foreign judgment on the merits when the rendering foreign court did not extend reciprocity to the forum court. France, where the doctrine originated, has abandoned it. EU law now expressly provides that "under no circumstances may a judgment given in a Member State be reviewed as to its substance" (Brussels Ia Regulation, Art. 52), and American courts have generally regarded foreign-country judgments to be as conclusive on the merits as sister-state judgments. Yet, as stated, violation of the recognizing forum's public policy is a defense to judgment recognition everywhere.

The problem, of course, is how to tell whether a foreign judgment offends local public policy without looking behind it to see what it stands for. The answer must be, at least in countries following the EU approach, that the recognizing court may act as if it were an appellate tribunal reviewing how the "lower court" decided the case. The judgment, *as rendered*, must be offensive. That matters are not clear cut in practice is touched upon in the next subsection. In the United States, the non-merger rule may make it easier to find that the judgment is offensive because of the cause of action that underlies it, while still not reviewing the way the foreign court arrived at its judgment.

---

[16]   Peter Hay, Patrick J. Borchers, Symeon C. Symeonides, & Christopher A. Whytock, *Conflict of Laws* § 24.3 (St. Paul, MN: West, 6th ed. 2018).

5.5.5.3   *Public policy and exporting forum values*

American courts have gone beyond considering the underlying cause of action (because of the non-merger rule) and the foreign judgment itself. They have, at least in one area, considered the content of the foreign law and the relevant foreign procedure, have found both offensive, and have therefore denied recognition of the resulting judgment. The type of case in point was English "libel tourism."

English law does not have the "public figure" defense of American libel law. This defense basically immunizes a defendant who makes otherwise libelous remarks about someone who is in the public eye, and reverses the ordinary burden of proof. Without the defense, the plaintiff *does not* have to prove that the remarks were false; the defendant may raise the truth of his or her statements as an affirmative defense, which is frequently quite difficult to prove. If a public figure defense were available, the plaintiff *would* have to prove that the remarks were false.[17] As a result of its plaintiff-friendly environment, England attracted libel actions – not only against English defendants, but also against foreigners who were in some way subject to English jurisdiction. Many of the resulting judgments were then sought to be enforced in the United States, where the judgment debtor had assets.

Some early American decisions refused recognition on American constitutional grounds. Later, the Federal "SPEECH Act" of 2010[18] made such treatment mandatory: A United States court, whether state or federal, must deny recognition to any foreign judgment issued by a jurisdiction that does not provide "at least as much protection for freedom of speech and press" as provided by the First Amendment to the United States Constitution.[19] The result goes beyond rejecting the foreign judgment's underlying cause of action in application of the non-merger law: It evaluates the content of the foreign law and the procedure applied by the forum's own standards. (Use of local standards was considered in the context of the "mirror image" rule in testing a foreign court's jurisdiction: see 5.5.2.2. However, once the foreign court had proper jurisdiction, there was no consideration of its law and procedure. See also note 15 above.)

---

[17]   *New York Times Co. v. Sullivan*, 376 U.S. 254, 279–80 (1964).
[18]   Securing the Protection of our Enduring and Established Constitutional Heritage Act.
[19]   28 U.S.C.A. § 4102 (West 2017).

The American "Bill of Rights" (the first ten amendments to the Federal Constitution) contains several guarantees besides freedom of speech. There is, for instance, the right to a jury trial, guaranteed in the Federal Constitution for some cases in federal courts, but also in state constitutions. When a court in a civil law country that does not use juries in civil cases renders a money judgment against a defendant, will such a judgment be denied recognition for failure to comply with the American right to a jury trial? No suggestion has gone this far, but the SPEECH Act does represent a (limited) return to *révision au fond*, combined with an export of American values.

The EU Court of Justice has also gone beyond the strict grounds for non-recognition of a judgment of an EU Member State court:[20] It held that the refusal of a French court to hear the defendant's counsel, unless the defendant would appear himself (and perhaps be subject to arrest), violated the defendant's right to defend. This enlarged slightly upon the ground for non-recognition when service is not made in time to prepare a defense (see 5.5.3): it concerned the ability of the defendant to defend. In American terms, it was a general "due process" ground.

5.5.6   No remedy available locally

In an early American decision,[21] recognition was denied to a Mexican judgment because it provided for periodic payments, and an American court (before the merger of law and equity jurisdiction) could only award a single monetary award – it could not establish and supervise an ongoing obligation. Today, with American courts having both common law and equity jurisdiction, the case would have come out otherwise. However, it does highlight a potential problem: What if the State A judgment gives a remedy, or decrees that a certain result shall be brought about, and these remedies or legal concepts are unknown to State B? Examples include the common law concept of future interests in real property law (see 4.6.2.5), as well as certain aspects of a common law trust (such as a settlor's power of appointment, and the rights of beneficiaries), both of which are unknown to the civil law, at least in the form known in the law of the country where the judgment or award was rendered. Following the early American case, recognition would have to be denied. To avoid

---

20   Case C-7/98, *Krombach v. Bamberski*, 2000 E.C.R. I-1935.
21   *Slater v. Mexican Nat'l R.R. Co.*, 194 U.S. 120 (1904).

such a result, both the EU's Brussels Ia and its Succession Regulations (Brussels Ia, Art. 54(1)) provide that the State A "order shall, to the extent possible, be adapted to a measure or an order known in the law of [State B] which has *equivalent effects attached to it and which pursues similar aims and interests* [as does State A law]".[22] Judicial inventiveness is called for. This is appropriate, in the interest of judicial cooperation and the free flow of otherwise valid judgments, to bring about what the State A court intended and the successful party had a right to expect. This appears to be a practical and fair solution to a problem when the alternative – denial of recognition – may require new litigation in State B in order to translate into money damages what the judgment creditor could not get in State B. Outside the EU, the situation is not that clear: Courts may be reluctant to adjust or adapt the State A judgment, thereby participating in the decision of the case. An unfortunate example is a Texas decision that denied a Mexican woman survivor rights as a widow of a common law marriage (see 3.6.2) because Mexico does not have such a marriage and Texas does not have a Mexican *concubinage* which would have given her rights under Mexican law.[23] The EU solution seems commendable.

5.6   The effect of a recognized judgment

5.6.1   The *res judicata* effect on the parties

When State A renders a judgment and State B recognizes it, does the judgment have the effect that it has in State A, or is it likened to one that State B would have rendered? On the face of it, the answer seems simple: Countries using the *exequatur* approach certify the State A judgment to be "enforceable" in State B, meaning enforceable as a judgment of State A, and not as one of State B. In American interstate practice, federal law requires that the recognizing state give sister-state judgments the same effect as they have in the state "from which they are taken," and American courts usually also accord the same effect (meaning: State A's) in the case of international judgments, albeit subject to additional defenses (see 5.5.2, 5.5.5). In EU law, Brussels Ia only states that another Member State's judgment "shall be recognized" (Art. 36(1)) but does not directly

---

22   Emphasis added.
23   *Nevarez v. Bailon*, 287 S.W.2d 521 (Tex. Civ. App. 1956).

address whether this shall be the State A or the State B effect. Article 54(1), discussed above (in 5.5.6), clarifies when it directs State B to adapt an unknown concept in the State A judgment to something similar in its own law. Again, the focus is on State A.

All this seems simple: It is the State A effect that is also to be implemented in State B. However, to comply with the directive fully, it is necessary to determine what the first judgment decided, that is, the extent to which the parties are bound. The *res judicata* effect of judgments (meaning, "the matter decided") differs among legal systems. It is perhaps the broadest in the American system: all that *was* raised and *could have been* raised in the proceeding (in which both parties participated) becomes *res judicata* when the case comes to judgment. Additional claims, counterclaims, or defenses arising from the same relationship that was before the court, but which were not raised, are lost because they *could have been* raised. In contrast, in many civil law systems, *res judicata* attaches only to that which was in fact raised before the court – to that which was actually litigated: matters that could have been raised in the first proceeding but were not, are not lost but can now be raised.

Consider the following example: In a civil law country, the losing party pays the court costs and the litigation expenses of both parties (e.g., attorneys' fees). For that reason, a cautious plaintiff may sue on only part of his or her claim, and if he or she wins, sue on the rest. Suing on the rest is not precluded because it was not previously before the first court. In the United States, each party pays its own costs (with statutory exceptions). An American plaintiff (who does not risk, upon a possible loss, having to pay the other side's expenses) must sue on his or her whole claim. If he or she sues only on a part, the rest will be lost.

What happens when a German plaintiff, having successfully recovered a first part of her claim in Germany, sues on the remaining part of her claim in an American court? The American *res judicata* rule would preclude a second (additional) recovery, but the German one would not. To be true to the "same effect as where rendered" directive (as it applies in American interstate cases), the American court should apply the German rule and permit the second claim to proceed. There is, however, dispute as to whether the American recognition rule extends to another country's *res judicata* rules.

Similarly, consider the effect of the (criticized) rule in American law, that the "merger rule" (see 5.5.5.2) does not apply to foreign-country judgments. Technically, this might mean that the foreign judgment creditor who is dissatisfied with his or her judgment could sue on the claim anew in the United States, even though he or she would be barred from doing so in the country of rendition. Once again, attention to the *res judicata* rules of the foreign country would avoid this result.

5.6.2   Effect on third parties

A judgment binds the parties to the suit. It may, of course, also have an indirect effect on non-parties, for instance when a court authorizes a new building project down the street. But can a non-party claim benefits from a judgment between other parties, or be directly prejudiced by one? Assume that an airline is sued by some of its passengers for damages resulting from an accident and loses. When other injured passengers from the same flight later sue for damages, may the airline defend itself anew, or is it barred from doing so ("estopped") because it lost in the earlier action? Some American courts have held that a party in the position of the airline is estopped, and have done so by applying their own estoppel law. This seems wrong: Again, the reach of a judgment (its effect and on whom) should be a matter of the first court's law.

If a plaintiff loses in a lawsuit, may someone in a like position still sue? In the above example, if the airline had won in the first suit, could other passengers still have sued, or would their suits be barred? An argument in favor of holding such suits barred was made by considering the first plaintiff to have been the "virtual representative" of others in like situations – an argument that the United States Supreme Court rightly rejected.[24] In the illustration, the other passengers, despite being in a like position, may bring their own suits. The Supreme Court decision acknowledged that non-parties can be bound when there is a legal relationship to a party (for instance, as a party's successor in a business enterprise), or when the non-party is a non-active member in a class action (i.e., did not exercise its right to opt out). Similarly, in the civil law, a judgment's effect on a non-party is narrowly circumscribed, indeed even more so, since class actions are available only in exceptional circumstances (see 3.4).

---

[24]   *Taylor v. Sturgell*, 553 U.S. 880 (2008).

5.7   Enforcement mechanisms

5.7.1   Foreign-country judgments in the United States

Earlier discussion (see 5.4.3) detailed that a foreign judgment (including a sister-state judgment) is enforced by suit on the foreign judgment in the local court, treating it as a claim. If successful, the result is a new local judgment. For sister-state judgments, expedited procedures are available in federal courts and on the basis of two uniform laws (which, however, subject the judgment holder to possible additional local defenses).

Similarly, recognition and enforcement of a foreign-country judgment primarily requires a suit on the judgment. Two uniform acts (an older one, from 1962, and a newer one, from 2005) also provide an expedited registration procedure, but are not in force in all states: the 2005 Act had been adopted by 40 states by 2022. Both acts have mandatory and discretionary provisions for non-recognition. Recognition is precluded by both if the foreign court lacked personal or subject matter jurisdiction, or if its legal system does not provide impartial tribunals or "procedures compatible with the requirements of due process of law [as defined by American standards]."[25]

The 2005 Act's discretionary grounds for non-recognition pick up standard objections (for instance, fraud in the procurement of the judgment), the existence of inconsistent judgments (see 5.5.4), violation of local public policy, lack of notice, and that the procedure followed by the foreign court in the particular case was incompatible with (American) due process standards. It is strange that lack of notice should be a discretionary ground when adequate notice is a due process requirement in interstate cases. Chances are that lack of notice will be subsumed under the due process incompatibility of the mandatory or discretionary grounds. The double reference to American due process standards raises the danger of the recognition process reverting to a *révision au fond* and an export of domestic values, as discussed in the context of the SPEECH Act of 2010 (see 5.5.5.3).

---

[25]   Uniform Foreign-Country Money Judgments Recognition Act § 4(b)(1) (2005). The earlier (1962) Act had identical language.

5.7.2   Recognition elsewhere

Other systems, whether they follow the civilian *exequatur* method for a declaration of enforceability or the more federal-like direct enforceability of Member State judgments of the EU, are much more limited in scope (because more specific), and the universal defense against recognition of a public policy violation provides additional leeway. In the EU, moreover, the EU rules apply to Member State judgments only, with members still free to resort to national rules with respect to non-EU state judgments, including, under German law, for example, the insistence on reciprocity (for which, see 5.5.2.2 and 5.5.5.1).

Within the EU, moreover, special provisions establish expedited procedures for a "European Payment Order for Uncontested Claims" and for "Small Claims" (under 10,000 euros). Such expedited procedures, streamlining recognition and enforcement and thereby unburdening courts, are lacking even in the American federal structure.

6 An assessment: tasks, developments, trends

6.1 In general

The past 50–70 years have seen major developments in the areas of international procedure and choice of law, roughly beginning with the American "conflicts revolution" in the 1950s, and in Europe with the 1968 Brussels Convention on Jurisdiction and the Enforcement of Judgments in Civil and Commercial Matters,[1] which ultimately became today's EU Brussels Ia Regulation. The intervening years saw the 1980 Rome Convention of the European Economic Community (EEC) on choice of law in contract (today, the EU's Rome I Regulation), the 1978 Hague Convention on the Law Applicable to Agency[2] (albeit in force in only four countries), the highly successful UNCITRAL Convention on the International Sale of Goods (CISG),[3] a number of successful Hague Conventions on family law issues and (since 2023) on the Recognition and Enforcement of Judgments in Civil or Commercial Matters,[4] and several further EU Regulations (e.g., on divorce and on succession). At the same time, a great many countries adopted new conflicts statutes or codified and expanded existing law. However, worldwide, even regional harmonization is still the exception; the most successful regional harmonization remains confined to the EU, EEA, and EFTA. National codifications often still adhere to aspects that do not further international cooperation (for instance, the reciprocity requirement in judgment recognition). The following highlights a few of

---

[1]   See 4.1.2.
[2]   See 4.1.1.
[3]   See 1.2.3.
[4]   See 6.2.1.

the areas in which further worldwide or regional harmonization would be beneficial, or to which national law might pay greater attention.

6.2 Jurisdiction and recognition of judgments in civil and commercial matters

6.2.1 Worldwide harmonization

In light of the success of the 1968 European Brussels Convention, the United States proposed in 1992 that the Hague Conference on Private International Law draft a Convention on the Recognition and Enforcement of Judgments that might find widespread acceptance among Member (and even non-Member) States. In the years that followed, agreement on acceptable jurisdictional bases proved a major stumbling block.

As earlier discussion detailed, countries differ with respect to the jurisdictional bases that they adopt for themselves and that they approve for the purpose of recognition of the judgments of others, with many favoring local plaintiffs in one way or another. When asked to recognize a foreign judgment, all states (except EU Member States, in most cases) review its jurisdictional basis; use of the "mirror image rule" might result in refusal to recognize.

All efforts failed, and work on the Convention was abandoned in 2005, save for one part of it, which is now the Hague Convention on Choice of Court Agreements (see 2.2.2). That Convention is in force in all 27 EU countries, Mexico, Montenegro, Singapore, and – following its decision to leave the EU ("Brexit") – the United Kingdom (since 2020). China, Israel, North Macedonia, Ukraine, and the United States have signed it but have not ratified it so far.

The Hague Conference began a new attempt in 2016, and a new Convention was proposed in 2019. It enters into force in 2023 in the European Union and Ukraine. As a result of Brexit, the European Union accession does not include the United Kingdom. The Convention has been signed by Costa Rica, Israel, the Russian Federation, the United States, and Uruguay but has not been ratified by any of them so far.

The Convention declares judgments as "eligible" for recognition if based on any of the bases of jurisdiction listed in it. The exorbitant bases that the EU Regulation prohibits are not on the list, but a state *may*, of course, continue to recognize such judgments under its national law. Consider the following illustration: Assume that the United States, the United Kingdom, and Belgium were contracting states to this Convention, and that the issue concerned recognition of an American judgment based on transient service (see 3.2.1). Such a judgment would not be "eligible" for recognition under the Convention in Belgium because transient service is not listed in the provision. However, the United Kingdom (if it should be a Convention partner) might still recognize a judgment under its national law (i.e., outside the Convention), since it also uses that jurisdictional basis. (See also 3.2.1 and 5.5.2.2.)

The eligibility list differs from EU law with respect to jurisdiction for claims arising from non-contractual obligations (mainly torts). The draft focusses on the place of acting, while EU law focusses on the place of injury or of acting, but under the Rome I Regulation, with respect to the applicable law, only on the place of injury. In view of this difference, Article 23(4) becomes important: the Convention does not apply if the law of a "Regional Economic Organization" (e.g., the European Union) had adopted different rules before the Convention entered into force.

If the Unites States should ratify the Convention in the future, another exception will be relevant. Article 22(2) excludes application of the Convention to judgment recognition cases between different legal systems within a contracting state. What does this mean? Since the United States has over fifty different, largely independent, legal systems within its federation, interstate judgment recognition issues are not subject to the Convention. This would distinguish the domestic effect of this Convention from the UNCITRAL (CISG) which, as federal law, overrides possible different or contrary provisions of contract law of the individual states, including the Uniform Commercial Code (UCC). An example of the latter is the writing requirement of the UCC (Statute of Frauds provision), while the CISG permits oral agreements.

The provision on refusal of recognition interestingly expands on the traditional public policy defense (see 5.5.5) in two respects. First, with respect to the requirement that the defendant must have received notice in time to defend, the draft adds that the second state might also base its refusal on service having been effected in a *manner* incompatible with its fundamental principles for service. This should permit refusal to recognize judgments where service was effected by *remise au parquet* (see 3.9). Second, several provisions, both in the context of eligibility and of recognition refusal, concern difficult aspects of patent, copyright, and trust matters.

Adoption by more countries of the Convention would be a major achievement, and also a promising one: It retains the leeway and flexibility that some states will no doubt require, while also establishing some ground rules, among them, that an "eligible" judgment "shall" be recognized, subject only to the Convention's grounds for refusal, and shall have the same effect as where rendered. The recognition mandate eliminates any consideration of reciprocity.

6.2.2   Arbitration

With respect to arbitral awards (not otherwise treated in this text), the 1958 New York Convention on the Recognition and Enforcement of Foreign Arbitral Awards has been highly successful. It is in force in 169 countries (in 2022) and thereby assures that arbitration – an increasingly important method for dispute resolution – will indeed result in awards entitled to virtually worldwide recognition, so long as its procedures are observed. Achieving agreement on this treaty, as well as on similar regional arrangements or new national laws (e.g., Ontario's of 2017[5]), was easier than it was for the original Hague Conference attempt with respect to judgments (see 6.2.1). Judgment recognition presupposes that the jurisdiction of the rendering state is acceptable to the recognizing state, as discussed. Arbitration does not involve similar jurisdictional problems: The New York Convention requires only that foreign arbitration, leading to the award to be recognized, be based on the parties' written agreement to arbitrate.

Arbitration is becoming increasingly important for the settlement of disputes between investors and the host state of their investments. The Convention on the International Center for Settlement of Investment Disputes (ICSID) was established in 1966 and now has 163 member countries (as of 2022). Its Article 54 provides that awards shall be recog-

---

[5]   International Commercial Arbitration Act, 2017, S.O. c. 2 (Can.).

nized and enforced in the contracting states. Since the Convention is not self-executing in the United States, implementing legislation provides that ICSID awards are to be given the same full faith and credit effect as judgments of the state courts of the United States.[6]

6.2.3 Regional harmonization

The most notable harmonization – indeed, unification – of jurisdiction and judgment recognition, of course, occurred in the EU, with respect to not only civil and commercial judgments, but also divorce, child custody, maintenance, succession, and insolvency. Other regional arrangements in South America and in the Commonwealth of Independent States extend mainly to civil and commercial matters, and participate with respect to other matters only in the framework of the Hague Conventions. Even with respect to civil and commercial matters, their instruments are (and function as) treaties, without the federal aspect enjoyed by EU law with its Court of Justice.

The comprehensive achievement of the EU Regulations, both with respect to international procedure and to choice of law, may be diminished by Brexit. The procedural Regulations, and even some aspects of the choice-of-law Regulations, apply only among Member States of the Union, which the United Kingdom ceased to be in 2019. Extension of EU rules between the EU and the United Kingdom by treaty (as the Brussels I Regulation was extended to Denmark) is a possibility, but there would be no jurisdiction of the EU Court of Justice, which the United Kingdom rejects. Another possibility is United Kingdom accession to the Lugano Convention (see 5.3.4). A new bilateral (EU–United Kingdom) agreement on some, but not all, aspects of the matters now covered by the Brussels and Rome Regulations appears as a third possibility. What the situation will ultimately be remains uncertain: that judicial cooperation will continue in some form seems assumed by all, although it will be far less cohesive than it is now.

---

6   22 USC §§ 1650, 1650a. For an important decision, see *Micula v. Government of Romania*, 404 F.Supp.3d 265 (D.D.C. 2019, aff'd 2022 WL 2281645 (D.C.Cir., June 24, 2022)). For the European Union, see also Alexander Yanos, "Intra-EU Investment Treaty Disputes in U.S. Courts," GAR, 2023 *Arbitration Review of the Americas* 87 (2022).

The 1979 Inter-American Convention on Extraterritorial Validity of Foreign Judgments and Arbitral Awards[7] (Montevideo Convention), sponsored by the Organization of American States, mandates recognition of judgments of contracting states but sets no jurisdictional standards of its own. Jurisdiction of the judgment-rendering state is judged by the recognizing state on the basis of its standards – perhaps a return to or retention of the "mirror image" rule (see 5.5.2.2). Furthermore, while 18 states signed the Convention, only 10 deposited instruments of ratification. Another Inter-American Convention (on Jurisdiction in the International Sphere for the Extraterritorial Validity of Foreign Judgments[8]), the La Paz Convention of 1984, does address the jurisdiction of the rendering court in a very limited way. It requires that the judgment debtor had his or her habitual residence or principal place of business in the judgment-rendering state. The Convention entered into force in 2004 on the basis of the ratification by two countries. There have been no additional ratifications.

As the EU experience continues to prove successful, and unification of international litigation-related law continues (as in the cases of succession and insolvency), other regions may opt for closer ties and harmonization of their laws. The current work on a draft for a new Hague Convention is an encouraging example.

6.2.4 National law

In 2005, the American Law Institute proposed a "Foreign Judgments and Enforcement Act" for possible adoption as a federal law. It would have made recognition of foreign-country judgments more difficult, for instance by reintroducing a reciprocity requirement that had been dropped by all but a handful of states since the early Supreme Court decision in *Hilton* (see 5.4.2). This proposal was not enacted, in part because of opposition by those reluctant to give up state control of foreign-country judgment recognition. Nevertheless, some tightening has taken place in the form of the 2010 SPEECH Act (see 5.5.5.3).

At the same time, the United States Supreme Court has tightened the limits of state court exercise of general jurisdiction ("doing business"). To

---

[7]   May 8, 1979, 1439 U.N.T.S. 87.
[8]   May 24, 1984, 24 I.L.M. 468 (1985).

soften the impact of this, the Court no longer requires that the defendant caused the harm in the forum in order to permit the exercise of specific jurisdiction, yet has stopped short of endorsing jurisdiction on "stream of commerce" grounds (see 3.2.2 and 3.3.2). Despite (and somewhat contradictory to) the foregoing, the exercise of (general) "transient jurisdiction" (see 3.2.1) remains permissible. Some of these changes may lessen objections to the enforcement of American judgments on jurisdictional grounds by other countries (except for transient jurisdiction). At the same time, the more limited exposure of a foreign defendant to suit in several American states also limits its exposure to the application of possibly unforeseen forum law (given the so often inward-looking American approach to choice of law (see 4.3.3.4 and 6.3) and often much higher American damage awards.

6.3 Choice of law

When there is uniform substantive law, there is no need for choice-of-law rules. The outstanding example is the (Vienna) CISG with 97 contracting states (in 2022), which provides substantive rules dealing with contract formation, performance, and breach. But not all contracting states have adopted all three parts of the Convention, and its rules do not apply to private (non-commercial) sales. What is more, some countries have made reservations, for instance regarding the need for a writing. The United States will only apply the Convention when the states involved are contracting states, and not when the other involved state is not a contracting state, but American conflicts rules refer to a third state which is a contracting party.

Hague Conventions can produce rules that could have virtually worldwide application, as shown by the current convention on judgment recognition. However, of the many Hague Conventions, only a few have succeeded in attracting a substantial number of ratifications. The Child Abduction and Intercountry Adoption Conventions are notable exceptions. The new Judgment Recognition Convention (2023) still awaits the accession of more countries in addition to those that have so far joined its adoption by the European Union.

There are also regional conventions, for instance among countries of the Organization of American States, addressing some specific issues (for instance, maintenance: see 5.3.2, 6.2.2), but also not covering all members.

All of the above are treaties. None has federal law-like character in structure and effect, as do the several EU Regulations. All of the latter are immediately binding law in the Member States that have not opted out (as some Regulations permit); they displace previous national conflicts rules (they are of "universal application"); and confer jurisdiction for binding interpretation on the EU Court of Justice. Many areas of private law are now covered by these Regulations, and more are sure to follow.

Much progress has been made by individual countries that have newly codified, or revised earlier codifications of, their conflicts law. One authoritative study details codification activity in 88 countries over a 50-year period.[9] Many of the newer ones draw on the EU experience: They retain the traditional (mainly civilian) rule-oriented approach but provide flexibility by specifying (in advance) circumstances in which departures from the basic rule may be warranted. Since a departure may address only a particular aspect of a case, *dépeçage* (see 4.3.4.2) may result more often than in the older civilian approach. Nevertheless, this *dépeçage* does not result from an issue-by-issue search for the applicable law, as under the American Second (and Draft Third) Restatements. Rather, it results from a value-based analysis, which is specifically envisioned to follow a formulated basic rule. An example, drawn from EU law, is the instruction that a court consider post-accident medical expenses incurred by the victim in his or her country of residence, and award damages in view of this inquiry, rather than only by the standards of the place of injury.

In the United States, the common law tradition of adherence to precedent has brought about some predictability, despite the non-specific approach to choice of law advocated by the Second Restatement. Nevertheless, conflicts law and international procedure remain the law of the individual states. Even "uniform laws" are state law; there is no national unity.

With respect to choice of law, the American Second Restatement has been followed by many states – by some only in part, by others more

---

9   Symeon C. Symeonides, *Codifying Choice of Law around the World* xxxv, 2 et seq. (Oxford: Oxford University Press, 2014).

extensively – but different approaches (such as comparative impairment: see 4.3.3.1) also continue to be followed. One problem in this area, as well as with regard to international procedure, is that American courts often treat international cases like interstate cases, thereby overlooking the fact that foreign parties conceive of and deal with the United States as a whole. As such, application of a particular state's (interstate) jurisdiction and conflicts law may not be anticipated. If it is, predictability can only be assured through use of choice-of-court and choice-of-law clauses. Lack of uniformity can also lead to forum shopping.

In 2014, the American Law Institute established a working group to draft a Restatement (Third) to replace the current one. Several commentators have urged more attention to international cases, as distinguished from interstate cases. In the drafts that have been produced as of 2022, inter-state jurisprudence (case law and commentary) continues to be central for the elaboration of some rules, and of the overall choice-of-law policy approach. Even the parties' contractual choice of the applicable law is given somewhat less effect than in other systems, particularly in the European Union.[10] More work will need to be done and more time will pass before the new Restatement (Third) will be promulgated, let alone before there can be any assessment of how the courts of the several states will receive and their case law reflect it.

---

[10] For an overview and commentary, see Peter Hay, "On the Road to a Third American Restatement of Conflicts Law," 42 IPRax 205 (2022).

Appendix: Sources of EU law

Procedural law

Regulation (EU) No. 1215/2012 on jurisdiction and the recognition and enforcement of judgments in civil and commercial matters, [2012] Official Journal L 351/1 ("Brussels Ia Regulation," also "Brussels I Recast"), amended by Regulation (EU) No. 542/2014, as regards the rules to be applied with respect to the Unified Patent Court and the Benelux Court of Justice, [2014] Official Journal L 163/1.

Regulation (EC) No. 2201/2003 concerning jurisdiction and the recognition and enforcement of judgments in matrimonial matters and the matters of parental responsibility, [2003] Official Journal L 338/1 ("Brussels IIa Regulation" or "Brussels II *bis*"), amended by Regulation (EC) No. 2116/2004, as regards treaties with the Holy See, [2004] Official Journal L 367/1; amended by Regulation (EU) on matrimonial matters, matters of parental responsibility and child abduction ("Brussels II *ter*") (effective August 1, 2022), [2019] Official Journal L 8214/2019.

Regulation (EU) No. 1103/2016 implementing enhanced cooperation in the area of jurisdiction, applicable law and the recognition and enforcement of decisions in matters of matrimonial property regimes, [2016] Official Journal L 183/1.

Regulation (EU) No. 1104/2016 – same as Regulation No. 1103/2016 concerning property consequences of registered partnerships, [2016] Official Journal L 183/30.

Regulation (EU) No. 848/2015 on insolvency procedures (recast), [2015] Official Journal L 141/19.

Regulation (EC) No. 1896/2006 creating a European payment procedure, [2006] Official Journal L 399/1.

Regulation (EU) No. 1784/2020 on service of judicial and extrajudicial documents in civil and commercial matters in EU countries, [2020] Official Journal L 405/40.

See also Convention on jurisdiction and the recognition and enforcement of judgments in civil and commercial matters, [2009] Official Journal L 147/5 ("Lugano Convention").

Applicable law

Regulation (EC) No. 593/2008 on the law applicable to contractual obligations, [2008] Official Journal L 177/6 ("Rome I Regulation").

Regulation (EC) No. 864/2007 on the law applicable to non-contractual obligations, [2007] Official Journal L 199/40 ("Rome II Regulation").

Regulation (EU) No. 1259/2010 implementing enhanced cooperation in the area of the law applicable to divorce and legal separation, [2010] Official Journal L 343/10 ("Rome III Regulation").

See also, *supra*, "Procedural law", Regulations (EU) 1103/2016, 1104/2016, and 848/2015.

See also, *infra*, "Maintenance obligations", and "Succession."

Maintenance obligations

Regulation (EC) No. 4/2009 on jurisdiction, applicable law, recognition and enforcement of decisions and cooperation in matters relating to maintenance obligations, [2009] Official Journal L 7/1, amended by Regulation (EC) No. 517/2013, [2013] Official Journal L 158/1.

Succession

Regulation (EU) No. 650/2012 on jurisdiction, applicable law, recognition and enforcement of decisions and acceptance and enforcement of authentic instruments in matters of succession and on the creation of a European Certificate Succession, [2012] Official Journal L 201/107.

Bibliography

American Law Institute (1972), *Restatement (Second) of Conflict of Laws.*

American Law Institute (2018), *Restatement (Fourth) of the Foreign Relations Law of the United States.*

Basedow, Jürgen (2015), *The Law of Open Societies – Private Ordering and Public Regulation in the Conflict of Laws* (The Hague: The Hague Academy of International Law).

Basedow, Jürgen, Giesela Rühl, Franco Ferrari, & Pedro de Miguel Asensio (eds.) (2017), *Encyclopedia of Private International Law*, 4 vols. (Northampton, MA and Cheltenham (UK): Edward Elgar Publishing).

Black, Vaughan & Stephen G.A. Pitel (2016), "Forum-Selection Clauses: Beyond the Contracting Parties," 12 J. Private Int'l L. 26.

Boele-Woelki, Katharina (2015), "Party Autonomy in Litigation and Arbitration in View of the Hague Principles on Choice of Law in International Commercial Contracts," 379 *Recueil des cours* 35.

Bogdan, Michael (2012), *Private International Law as Component of the Law of the Forum*, Pocket series of General Courses (Hague Academy of International Law).

Borchers, Patrick J. (1990), "The Death of Constitutional Law of Personal Jurisdiction: From Pennoyer to Burnham and Back Again," 24 U.C. Davis L. Rev. 19.

Borchers, Patrick J. (2005), "Flexibility and Predictability: The Emergence of Near-Universal Choice of Law Principles," in Rasmussen-Bonne, Freer, Lüke et al. (eds.), *Balancing of Interests – Festschrift für Peter Hay* 49 (Frankfurt am Main: Verlag Recht und Wirtschaft).

Borchers, Patrick J. (2008), "Categorical Exceptions to Party Autonomy in Private International Law," 82 Tul. L. Rev. 1645.

Borchers, Patrick J. (2011), "J. McIntyre Machinery, Goodyear, and the Incoherence of the Minimum Contacts Test," 44 Creighton L. Rev. 1245.

Borchers, Patrick J. (2016), "An Essay on Predictability in Choice-of-Law Doctrine and Implications for a Third Conflicts Restatement," 49 Creighton L. Rev. 495.

Borchers, Patrick J. (2016), *Conflicts in a Nutshell* (6th ed., St. Paul, MN: West Publishing).

Borchers, Patrick J. (2021), "*Ford Motor Co. v. Eighth Judicial District Court* and 'Corporate Tag Jurisdiction' in the Pennoyer Era," 72 Case W.L. Rev. 45.

Cheshire, North, & Fawcett (2017), *Private International Law*, edited by Toremans et al. (15th ed., Oxford: Oxford University Press).

Coyle, John F. (2017), "The Cannons of Construction of Choice-of-Law Clauses," 92 Wash. L. Rev. 631.

Cuniberti, Gilles (2017), *Conflict of Laws: A Comparative Approach – Text and Cases* (Northampton, MA and Cheltenham (UK): Edward Elgar Publishing).

Currie, Brainerd (1959), "Notes on Methods and Objectives in the Conflict of Laws," 1959 Duke L.J. 171.

Currie, Brainerd (1963), *Selected Essays on the Conflict of Laws* (Durham, NC: Duke University Press).

DeBoer, T.M. (1987), *Beyond Lex Loci* (Deventer: Kluwer).

Dicey, Morris, & Collins (2022), *The Conflict of Laws* (16th ed., London: Sweet and Maxwell).

Dickinson, Andrew (2016), "The UK's EU Exit and the Conflict of Laws," 12 J. Private Int'l L. 194.

Elbati, Béligh (2017), "Reciprocity and the Recognition and Enforcement of Foreign Judgments: A Lot of Bark But Not Much Bite," 13 J. Private Int'l L. 184.

Einhorn, Talia (2022), *Private International Law in Israel* (3rd. ed., Kluwer).

Fazilatfar, Hossein (2019), *Overriding Mandatory Rules in International Commercial Arbitration* (Northampton, MA and Cheltenham (UK): Edward Elgar Publishing).

Ferrari, Franco & Diego P. Fernández Arroyo (eds.) (2019), *Private International Law: Contemporary Challenges and Continuing Relevance* (Northampton, MA and Cheltenham (UK): Edward Elgar Publishing).

Freer, Richard D. (2022), *Civil Procedure*, Aspen Student Treatise Series (5th ed., Wolters Kluwer).

Hay, Peter (1990), "Transient Jurisdiction, Especially over International Defendants: Critical Comments on *Burnham v. Superior Court*," 1990 U. Ill. L. Rev. 593.

Hay, Peter (1991), "Flexibility versus Predictability and Uniformity in Choice of Law – Reflections on Current European and United States Conflicts Law," 226 *Recueil des cours* 281.

Hay, Peter (2012), "Reviewing Foreign Judgments in American Practice – Conclusiveness, Public Policy, and Révision au fond," in Reinhold Geimer and Rolf A. Schütze (eds.), *Festschrift für Kaissis* 365 (Munich: Sel, Sellier Law Publishers).

Hay, Peter (2013), "Notes on the European Union's Brussels-I 'Recast' Regulation – An American Perspective," 2013 Eu L. F. 1.

Hay, Peter (2015), "European Conflicts Law after the American 'Revolution'," 2015 Eu L. F. 1 and 2015 U. Ill. L. Rev. 2053.

Hay, Peter (2017), "The United States: The Use and Determination of Foreign Law in Civil Litigation in the United States," in Yuko Nishitani (ed.), *Treatment of Foreign Law: Dynamics towards Convergence?*, Ius Comparatum – Global Studies in Comparative Law, Vol. 26, (Berlin: Springer Verlag), 397–427, reprinted in (2014) 62 Am. J. Comp. L. Supp. 213.

Hay, Peter (2020), "Forum Selection Clauses – Procedural Tools or Contractual Obligations?", 40 IPRax 505.

Hay, Peter (2021), "Piercing the Corporate Veil in American Procedural Law," in Boris Paal et al. (eds), *Deutsches, Europäisches und Vergleichendes Wirtschaftsrecht – Festschrift für Ebke* 337 (Munich, C.H. Beck Verlag).

Hay, Peter (2022), "On the Road to a Third American Restatement of Conflicts Law," 42 IPRax 205.

Hay, Peter (2023) *Conflict of Laws – Black Letter Outlines* (9th ed., St. Paul, MN: West Academic Publishing 2023).

Hay, Peter, Patrick J. Borchers, & Richard D. Freer (2021), *Conflict of Laws – Private International Law: Cases and Materials* (16th ed., St. Paul, MN: Foundation Press).

Hay, Peter, Patrick J. Borchers, Symeon C. Symeonides, & Christopher A. Whytock (2018), *Conflict of Laws* (6th ed., St. Paul, MN: West Publishing Co.).

Juenger, Friedrich K. (1983), "General Course on Private Int'l Law," 193 *Recueil des cours* 119.

Juenger, Friedrich K. (1984), "Conflict of Laws: A Critique of Interest Analysis," 32 Am. J. Comp. L. 1.

Juenger, Friedrich K. (1993), *Choice of Law and Multistate Justice* (Dordrecht, Boston, MA, London: Martinus Nijhoff Publishers).

Kegel, Gerhard (1964), "The Crisis of Conflict of Laws," 112 *Recueil des cours* 91.

Kegel Gerhard & Klaus Schurig (2004), *Internationales Privatrecht* (9th ed., Munich: C.H. Beck Verlag).

Kramer, Malte, Christian Baldus, & Martin Schmidt-Kessel (eds.) (2017), *Brexit und die juristischen Folgen* (Baden-Baden: Nomos).

Kramme, Malte (2021), Private Divorce in Light of the Recast Brussels IIbis Regulation, *Zeitschrift für das internationale Privatrecht der Europäischen Union* No. 3/2021, 101.

Kruger, Thalia (2016), "The Quest for Legal Certainty in International Civil Cases," 380 *Recueil des cours* 281.

Leible, Stefan (ed.) (2016), *General Principles of European Private International Law* (Netherlands: Wolters Kluwer).

Magnus, Ulrich and Peter Mankowski (2022), *Brussels Ibis Regulation* (2nd ed., Köln: Verlag Otto Schmidt KG).

Morris, J.H.C. (1973), "Law and Reason Triumphant or How Not to Review a Restatement," 21 Am. J. Comp. L. 322, 324.

Morris, P. Sean (2016), "The Modern Transplantation of Continental Law in England: How English Private International Law Embraced Europeanization, 1972–2014," 12 J. Int'l Private L. 587.

Nishitani, Yuko (ed.) (2017), *Treatment of Foreign Law: Dynamics towards Convergence?, Ius Comparatum* – Global Studies in Comparative Law, Vol. 26 (Berlin: Springer Verlag).

Rabel, Ernst (1958), *The Conflict of Laws – A Comparative Study* (2nd ed., prepared by Ulrich Drobnig, Ann Arbor, MI: University of Michigan Press).

Reimann, Mathias (2016), "Choice of Law Codification in Modern Europe: The Costs of Multi-Level Law-Making," 49 Creighton L. Rev. 507.

Roosevelt III, Kermit (1999), "The Myth of Choice of Law: Rethinking Conflicts," 97 Mich. L. Rev. 97 (I), 2448 (II).

Roosevelt III, Kermit (2019), "Certainty versus Flexibility in the Conflict of Laws," in Franco Ferrari and Diego P. Fernández Arroyo (eds.), *Private International Law: Contemporary Challenges and Continuing Relevance* (Northampton, MA and Cheltenham (UK): Edward Elgar Publishing), at 6.

Siehr, Kurt (2005), "General Problems of Private International Law in Modern Codifications," VII Yearbook of Private Int'l L. 17.

Sold, Jena A. (2011), "Inappropriate Forum or Inappropriate Law? A Choice of Law Solution to the Jurisdictional Standoff with Latin America," 60 Emory L.J. 1437.

Symeonides, Symeon C. (2009), "Oregon's New Choice-of-Law Codification for Tort Conflicts: An Exegesis," 88 Oregon L. Rev. 963.

Symeonides, Symeon C. (2014), *Codifying Choice of Law Around the World* (Oxford: Oxford University Press).

Symeonides, Symeon C. (2016), *Oxford Commentaries on American Law: Choice of Law* (Oxford: Oxford University Press).

Symeonides, Symeon C. (2017), "Choice of Law in the American Court in 2016: Thirtieth Annual Survey," 65 Am. J. Comp. L. No. 2.

Symeonides, Symeon C. (2017), "Private International Law: Idealism, Pragmatism, Eclecticism," 384 *Recueil des cours* 30.

Symposium (2012), "Personal Jurisdiction in the Twenty-First Century: The Implications of McIntyre and Goodyear" (contributions by Miller, Steiman, Vail, Stein, Freer, Silberman, Brilmayer/Smith, Arrington, Citron, Feder, Peddle, Perdue, & Stravitz) 63 S.C. L. Rev. 436.

Weintraub, Russell J. (1994), "Choosing Law with an Eye on the Prize," 15 Mich. J. Int'l L. 471.

Weintraub Russell J (2008), "Choice-of-Law Rule of the European Community Regulation on the Law Applicable to Non-Contractual Obligations: Simple and Predictable, Consequences-Based, or Neither?," 43 Tex. Int'l L.J. 401.

Weintraub, Russell J. (2010), *Commentary on the Conflict of Laws* (6th ed., New York, NY: Foundation Press).

Weller, Mattias (2017), "Choice of Forum Agreements under the Brussels I Recast and the Hague Convention: Coherence and Clashes," 13 J. Private Int'l L. 91.

Whytock, Christopher A. (2011), "The Evolving Forum Shopping System," 96 Cornell L. Rev. 48.

Whytock, Christopher A. & Cassandra Burke Robertson (2011), "Forum Non Conveniens and the Enforcement of Foreign Judgments," 111 Colum. L. Rev. 1444.

Xu, Qingkun (2017), "The Codification of Conflicts Law in China: A Long Way to Go," 65 Am. J. Comp. L. 919.

Yanos, Alexander (2022), "Intra-EU Investment Treaty Disputes in US Courts," in Global Arbitration Review, *The Arbitration Review of the Americas 2023*, 87.

Yntema, Hessel (1957), "The Objectives or Private International Law," 35 Can. Bar Rev. 721.

Index

Social Policy
Second Edition
Daniel Béland and Rianne Mahon

Substantive Criminal Law
Stephen J. Morse

Cross-Border Insolvency Law
Reinhard Bork

Behavioral Finance
H. Kent Baker, John R. Nofsinger, and Victor Ricciardi

Critical Global Development
Uma Kothari and Elise Klein

Private International Law and
Procedure
Second Edition
Peter Hay

Victimology
Sandra Walklate

Party Politics
Richard S. Katz

Contract Law and Theory
Brian Bix

Environmental Impact
Assessment
Second Edition
Angus Morrison-Saunders

Tourism Economics
David W. Marcouiller

Service Innovation
*Faïz Gallouj, Faridah Djellal, and
Camal Gallouj*

U.S. Disability Law
Peter Blanck